SHIISM AND POLITICS IN THE MIDDLE EAST

COMPARATIVE POLITICS AND INTERNATIONAL STUDIES SERIES

Series editor, Christophe Jaffrelot

This series consists of translations of noteworthy manuscripts and publications in the social sciences written by the foremost French researchers, from Sciences Po, Paris.

The focus of the series is the transformation of politics and society by transnational and domestic factors—globalisation, migration, and the postbipolar balance of power on the one hand, and ethnicity and religion on the other. States are more permeable to external influence than ever before and this phenomenon is accelerating processes of social and political change the world over. In seeking to understand and interpret these transformations, this series gives priority to social trends from below, as much as to the interventions of state and non-state actors.

LAURENCE LOUËR

Shiism and Politics in the Middle East

Translated from the French by
John King

HURST & COMPANY, LONDON

First published by Les Editions Autrement, Paris, as *Chiisme et politique au Moyen-Orient. Iran, Irak, Liban, Monarchies Du Golfe*, Copyright © 2008, Editions Autrement

First published in the United Kingdom in 2012 by
C. Hurst & Co. (Publishers) Ltd.,
41 Great Russell Street, London, WC1B 3PL
Translation copyright © 2012 by C. Hurst & Co. (Publishers) Ltd.
All rights reserved.
Printed in India

The right of Laurence Louër to be identified as the author of this publication is asserted by her in accordance with the Copyright, Designs and Patents Act, 1988.

A Cataloguing-in-Publication data record for this book is available from the British Library.

ISBN: 978-1-84904-202-4

This book is printed using paper from registered sustainable and managed sources.

www.hurstpub.co.uk

CONTENTS

Transcription of Arabic and Persian Names
and Expressions   vii
Glossary   ix

Introduction. Shiism: The Key to Regional Realignment   1

1. The Clergy: A Key Element   5
   The training and organisation of the clergy   6
   Najaf and Qom: Shiism's twin cradles   7
   The clergy and politics: Permanent revolution?   11
   Shia Political Islam at the heart of the clerical
   institution in Iraq   14
   Factional quarrels   16
   The Iranian clergy and the state   19
   Clergy and laity: A "structuring cleavage"   22

2. Transnational Networks   27
   Al-Da'wa on the national and transnational plane   28
   The Najaf connection in Lebanon and Bahrain   29
   The marja'iyya and the merchant notability of
   the Gulf   33
   Suppression and exile   37
   The Shirazists: The other transnational network   39
   Musa al-Sadr in Lebanon: A family story   45

3. The Islamic Republic of Iran: A Disputed Model   51
   The export of the revolution by the Shirazists   52

CONTENTS

Iran's policy in Lebanon: The birth of Hezbollah	55
Hezbollah as a transnational network	60
Iranian foreign policy and the Shia movements	66
The Shia movements and quarrels within the marja'iyya	71
Iran: The pros and the antis	79
4. The Post Saddam Era	83
The Iraqi Shia movements and Iran from 2003: From ideology to tactics	85
The reasons for conflict between Sunnis and Shias in Bahrain	94
The Shias as supporters of the throne in Saudi Arabia	105
Lebanon: The stumbling block for the dynamic of domestification?	113
Conclusion: Towards The Secularisation of Shia Political Islam	125
The gap widens between clerics and laymen	126
The marja'iyya in politics	130
The rise of millenarianism	135
Notes	141
Bibliography	147
Index	151

TRANSCRIPTION OF ARABIC AND PERSIAN NAMES AND EXPRESSIONS

A simplified transcription of Arabic and Persian has been employed. The letters "ain" and "hamza" are not transcribed, except where it seemed essential, for example in the name of the Iraqi al-Da'wa party. Words have not in general been Anglicised, except for certain very well known names such as Hassan and Hussein. Certain Persian expressions have been given in their Arabic form, as have some proper names. For instance, the choice was made to write *wilayat al-faqih* and not *vilayat-e faqih*, and to put Ali al-Sistani, not Ali Sistani. The decision was not always simple, as there is widespread interpenetration between the Arab and Persian worlds in the linguistic as well as the demographic sphere. Consistency has been the goal. Words for religious concepts have been given in Arabic form, this was because they derive from Arabic and were most often initially formulated in Arabic, even by the Iranians themselves. Proper names have been given in their Arabic form when they relate to persons who reside in Arab countries or whose activity and influence is mainly in the Arab world. Singular and plural forms of Arabic words have been given where appropriate, with the exception that the plural of *effendi* (already a non-standard spelling) has been given as *effendis*.

GLOSSARY

Ahl al-bayt — Literally, "the people of the house", that is to say, the members of the family of the Prophet Mohammed.

Alim (pl. *ulama*) — Literally, a "scholar": the expression is used more specifically to refer to religious scholars.

Ashura — Literally, "the tenth": a celebration that takes place on the tenth day of the Muslim month of Muharram to commemorate the martyrdom of the Imam Hussein in 680 at Karbala. It is marked by processions of men dressed in black who flagellate themselves with whips as a sign of penitence.

Ayatollah — Literally, "The Sign of God". This is a title which applies to Shia religious scholars who have attained the level of *ijtihad*.

Effendi — In the Arab world in the later nineteenth century, this Ottoman expression was used to designate literate and westernised city dwellers, by contrast with the clergy. Within the Shia Islamic movement, especially in Iraq and the Gulf, it is used today to refer to a lay

GLOSSARY

	(i.e. non-clerical) official from a Shia Islamic organisation.
Faqih (pl. *fuqaha*)	A religious scholar who specialises in *fiqh*, i.e. Islamic law.
Fatwa (pl. *fatawa*)	A religious opinion given by a *marja'* on a point of doctrine.
Hawza (*hawza 'ilmiyya*)	Literally, the "Territory of Knowledge". In a general sense, this expression designates the community of religious professors and students. More specifically, it refers either to the collectivity of religious seminaries in a particular place, or to a particular religious teaching institution.
Hezbollah	Literally, the "Party of God". In a general sense the expression refers to those who identify themselves with the political and religious ideas of Ruhollah Khomeini. More specifically, it designates certain Shia Islamic movements.
Hujjat al-islam	Literally "The Proof of God". This is an honorary title accorded by Shias to scholars who have not attained the level of *ijtihad*.
Husseini	An adjective deriving from the name of Hussein, the third Imam. In contrast with the adjective *hassani* (from the name Hassan), this adjective refers to a position of commitment, most often of a revolutionary nature, in political affairs.
Husseiniyya (pl. *husseiniyyat*)	A place devoted to the celebration of the festival of Ashura, as well as other Shia festivals. It also serves as a meeting place for marriages and funerals.
Ijtihad	The independent interpretation of religious texts; the capacity to offer such interpretation.

GLOSSARY

Imam (pl. *a'ima*)	Literally, "Guide". This is a term which has many connotations within Shiism. On the one hand, it is used to designate the twelve infallible Imams. It also refers to those who lead prayer in the mosques. Finally, it may be used as a title when referring to a person who has played a major religious or political role.
Ja'fari	This term designates the Shia school of Islamic law, which was codified for the Shias by the sixth Imam, Ja'far al-Sadiq.
Khums (pl. *akhmas*)	Literally, "a fifth part". This is a religious tax consisting of one fifth of the surplus annual income of a family after expenses necessary for subsistence have been paid. Half is payable to the *marja'* and half to the *sada*.
Mahdi	Literally, "The Rightly Guided". This refers to the twelfth Imam, who after being occulted by God from the sight of men is supposed to return at the End of Time to impose justice and truth.
Marja' (*al-taqlid*) (pl. *maraji' al-taqlid*)	Literally, the "Source of Emulation", in other words the supreme religious authority to whom Shias should refer in matters of religious doctrine.
Mujtahid (pl. *mujtahidin*)	A religious scholar capable of *ijtihad*.
Pasdar (pl. *pasdaran*)	This is a Persian term that refers in an abbreviated form to members of the Guardians of the Revolution in Iran (*sepah-e pasdaran-e enqelab-e islami*). The *pasdaran* are a military formation, directly under the authority of the Guide of the Revolution, whose function is the protection of the revolution against

GLOSSARY

	counter-revolutionaries. They also serve, however, as an essential instrument of Iranian foreign policy, in particular through their role in the export of the revolution and the training of activists in the Shia Islamic movements.
Sayyid (pl. s*ada*)	Descendants of the Prophet Mohammed.
Umma	A term which refers to the Muslim community as a whole.
Wali amr al-muslimin	Literally, "The Leader of the Muslims". This is one of the titles of the Guide of the Revolution in Iran, and indicates his claim to rule not only the Iranians but also all Muslims.
Waqf (pl. *awqaf*)	A bequest left in trust in perpetuity to an Islamic institution.
Wilayat al-faqih	Literally, the "Authority of the Doctor of the Law". This doctrine was developed by Ruhollah Khomeini and stipulates that during the period in which the twelfth Imam is occulted from view, the Imam's political powers and in particular the government of the state may be legitimately exercised by religious scholars.

INTRODUCTION

SHIISM: THE KEY TO REGIONAL REALIGNMENT

The overthrow of the regime of Saddam Hussein in April 2003 led to a radical upheaval in the geopolitical equilibriums of the Middle East. A theme emerges from most commentaries attempting to describe the new regional situation: namely, the return of the Shias in force to the centre stage, a phenomenon known as the "Shia revival"[1] or the "Shia crescent".[2] In practice, the end of the Baathist regime in Iraq allowed the Shia Islamic movements to take power, in a country where Shias make up close to 60 per cent of the population, and where the weakness of the great inter-communal parties empowered movements that laid claim to a particular religious or national identity. In addition, the fall of Saddam Hussein, coupled with the collapse of the Taliban in Afghanistan, provided a historic and unexpected opportunity for the Islamic Republic of Iran, where Shiism is the state religion, to achieve the status of a regional power, as had been its ambition since the revolution of 1979. As part of Iran's bid for hegemony, its possible acquisition of nuclear weapons will be a key issue in the coming years. In the short term, however, the most reliable means by which Iran can exercise its influence remains its ability to intervene in theatres of action, such as Lebanon, that are sometimes far from its frontiers, through the instrumentalisation of Shia Islamic movements.

Such movements exist in most regions of Shia population, from the Arab world to India and Central Asia, though the paucity of studies of recent developments in Shia Islam has so far made it difficult to compile a general survey. In the 1980s, the decade following the revolution in Iran, a number of books on this subject were published. The majority of these, however, concentrated on a single country, for the most part Iran itself, Iraq, or Lebanon; or were collective studies with chapters each devoted to the study of one specific movement or another. None has so far offered a framework for comprehensive analysis that would allow local specificities to be taken into account whilst also emphasising common underlying elements. This is what this book will attempt. It will not, however, look at the Shia world in its entirety but will focus rather on those Arab countries in which the Shia Islamic movements have played, and continue to play, a key role in the internal political process. These are Iraq, Lebanon, and some of the Gulf monarchies (Saudi Arabia, Bahrain, Kuwait, the United Arab Emirates and Oman). Central to the Shia question in each of these countries is the thorny issue of relations with Iran. The Islamic revolution created a centripetal dynamic, establishing Iran not merely as the political reference point for most Shia Islamic movements, but also as the sanctuary for a host of militants who dreamed of putting an end to the rule of illegitimate governments. An appreciation of what remains of this force of attraction today, more than thirty years after the Islamic revolution, is crucial for an understanding of the political trajectory of the Shia Islamic movements in all its complexity.

It has, for some years, been conventional to assume that the Arab and Iranian Shia communities constitute two mutually antagonistic entities.[3] The decision by the United States to depose Saddam Hussein was predicated on the assumption of this stark antithesis. It was assumed that under the moderate leadership of Ayatollah Sistani, the Iraqi Shias would shun Iran's

INTRODUCTION

political model and would not permit themselves to be subjugated. On the contrary, it was thought that they would become an alternative to the Islamic Republic and a centre of Shia influence that would rival Iran. In short, the elevation of the Shias to power in Baghdad would be the best means to weaken Iran. The restriction of this study to the Arab world should not be taken as an endorsement of this assessment. Rather, the aim will be to demonstrate directly the extent to which any attempt at an analysis of Shia political Islam, or indeed of Shiism in general, based on the perspective of a supposedly atavistic antagonism between Arabs and Iranians, would be illusory. Most of the actors we shall follow move easily between the Arab and Iranian worlds, illustrating that the respective nationalist positions, predicated on the notion of inherent antagonism, conceal the profound interpenetration of these two worlds.

For these reasons, the decision to focus on the Arab world is arbitrary, reflecting simply the requirement, in the interests of presenting an analysis that accounts for local issues in the light of general considerations, to achieve a better understanding through not attempting too much, therefore focusing on familiar territory. This is, incidentally, the reason for the use of the Arabic versions of certain terms and personal names that are often given in their Persian equivalents elsewhere, but which in our field of study are used in Arabic by the actors themselves. Another limitation of the subject matter of this book, imposed on empirical grounds and in contrast to other works, is that we shall confine our analysis to those Shias known as "Twelvers", ignoring such minority Shia movements as Zaidism, Ismailism, the Alawites and the Druzes.[4]

What, in fact, is Shiism? First of all, it is a legitimist movement, which, in contrast to the Sunnis, asserts that the Prophet Mohammed specifically said that his successors should be from the lineage of Ali, his cousin and his daughter Fatima's husband. In addition, for the Shias, those they refer to as the

"Imams", that is to say Ali and his descendants, have access to the hidden meaning of the divine message, and are endowed with religious infallibility. It is from this that they derive their political legitimacy. For the "Twelver" Shias, who constitute the great majority, there are twelve Imams. The twelfth, the Mahdi, did not die but was occulted by God from the sight of mankind and will return at the "End of Days" to impose justice and truth. However, the reign of the Imams was beset by numerous quarrels over succession, which lay at the origin of the various heterodox movements mentioned above. From a doctrinal standpoint, most of these have little in common today with Twelver Shiism. They also exist within socio-political contexts, which are radically exceptional and make any assessment of their situation in terms similar to those appropriate to the Twelver Shias irrelevant. For this reason, neither Syria nor Yemen will be discussed in this book.

1

THE CLERGY

A KEY ELEMENT

The majority of the Shia Islamic movements currently active were founded by and are run by clerics. Shia clerics are recognisable by their distinctive dress, which consists of a long cloak (*abaya*) and, more particularly, a turban, coloured black for those entitled to use the title *sayyid*, the descendants of the Prophet Mohammed, and white for those who are unable to claim such prestigious ancestry. The presence of clerics at the highest level in the structures of command is without question a characteristic distinctive of the Shia version of political Islam. Sunni political Islam, both in its ideology and in terms of its social base, was from the outset built up in opposition to the traditional religious "establishment", which it views as having been appropriated by impious governments, and considers as responsible for the decline of Islam. The development of Shia political Islam, by contrast, is inextricably bound up with that of the clergy though there are also anti-clerical currents within it. It can only be understood through the examination of the workings of the clerical institution (the *hawza*) and especially of the concept of religious authority (*marja'iyya*).

SHIISM AND POLITICS IN THE MIDDLE EAST

The training and organisation of the clergy

In contrast to the orthodox doctrine of the Sunnis, for whom there is no intermediary between God and his believers, Shiism quickly posited the need for a body of religious professionals: a clergy in the full sense. After the occultation of the twelfth Imam in the ninth century, it was logical that the religious scholars—the *ulama*—would come to play a central role. At that moment, they became the representatives of the missing Imam, filling the vacuum created by the absence of religious leadership. In his name, they raised taxes and administered justice. While they did not claim religious infallibility, they perfected a science of the interpretation of texts, which would enable them to formulate new religious doctrines adapted to historical changes.

There is a question, however, as to what are the temporal powers of the Imam, who, ideally, is not only a religious guide but also the sole legitimate political leader. Until Ruhollah Khomeini (1901–1989) formulated the doctrine of *wilayat al-faqih* in 1970, which bestowed upon the clergy the right to govern the state, it was accepted that clerical leadership should be limited to the spiritual sphere. It was over precisely this point that Khomeini would prove to be "revolutionary".

Throughout history, the Shia *ulama* have tended to congregate in geographical regions where the authority of the Caliphate was weak. This was so, for instance, in the case of the mountainous zone of Jabal Amil, situated in present-day southern Lebanon, and also for the historic territory of Bahrain, which included among other elements the contemporary state of Bahrain together with the eastern province of Saudi Arabia. In such regions, they quickly established states and political entities founded on the basis of revolt against the Sunni caliphs, the leaders of which appealed to the legitimacy associated with the lineage of Ali and Fatima. At the end of the ninth century, the Carmathians, an Ismaili sect, established within the historic territory of Bahrain, a state that was particularly antagonistic

THE CLERGY: A KEY ELEMENT

towards the Caliphate, as well as developing a prototype welfare state and fostering a high level of religious exegesis. Before its overthrow in 1075, the Carmathian state helped firmly to entrench the Ismaili faith within the historical territory of Bahrain, whilst also contributing to the establishment of a class of highly energetic Twelver Shia *ulama* who in the end imposed orthodox Shiism in the region.[1]

It was also natural that the Shia *ulama* should find a foothold in territories under the rule of Shia dynasties, such as the Buyids, who ruled in Baghdad between 945 and 1055, and especially the Safavids (1501–1722) who installed Shiism as the state religion in Iran. In order to convert their subjects, who were at the time principally Sunnis, to the doctrine whose armed champions they had become, the Safavids imported religious scholars from Jabal Amil and historic Bahrain. Tasked with endowing the new regime with legitimacy, they developed Shia doctrine and ritual, while refining the process of recruitment to the clerical hierarchy which thus developed the necessary critical mass. This era saw the first appearance of certain of the striking titles adopted by clerics still employed today, such as *hujjat al-islam* (proof of Islam) or *ayatollah* (sign of God), the appellation of the most advanced scholars. Iran at that time became the incontestable religious and political centre of the Shia world, and it was during the Safavid era that Shiism became a defining feature of the Iranian state.

Najaf and Qom: Shiism's twin cradles

In the eighteenth century, the Safavid dynasty fell under the onslaught of Sunni invaders from Afghanistan. After the final expulsion of the invaders and the restoration of order, the new dynasty that came to power—the Afsharids (1736–1795)—took it upon itself to dilute the Shia specificity of the state, severing at the same time its privileged relationship with the religious scholars. Many of the *ulama* took the decision to go into exile, either in Mesopotamia (present-day Iraq) or in the Indian sub-continent. It was thus Mesopotamia, the site of the tombs of a number of the Imams, including that of Ali in Najaf and of Hussein in Karbala, that became over time a new focus of attraction for the clergy. Southern Mesopotamia was at that time a frontier zone between the Ottoman and Iranian Empires, which regularly clashed over its control. Though formally under Ottoman sovereignty, the holy cities where the scholars had taken refuge were in fact largely autonomous, run by clerical mafias that, whilst exploiting the inhabitants, also preserved their independence against all attempts by the central government to intervene.

What took place in this period is of crucial importance in understanding subsequent developments. In Mesopotamia, the Shia clergy abandoned its status as a state religious body, setting itself up instead as an extraterritorial authority virtually independent of any state. Under the Qajar dynasty (1781–1925), which reinstated Shiism as the state religion in Iran and attempted to use the clergy as a bridgehead for its influence within the Ottoman Empire, the Iranian state continued to be an important source of finance for the clergy in Mesopotamia. Jealous of its independence, however, the clergy preferred to turn for support to civil society. The *khums*, the tax levied by the religious scholars on the faithful, equivalent to one fifth of a family's annual income after the deduction of necessary living expenses, was a key element in this novel system of financial provision. The result was that proselytism was no longer simply an act of piety but also a material necessity; the more Shias there were, the greater the means at the disposal of the clergy for its survival and development. This accounted for the zeal with which the conversion of the tribes of southern Mesopotamia was undertaken in the nineteenth century and the conversion to Shiism of a majority of the population of contemporary Iraq. The proselytisation of the *ulama* fell on fertile soil amongst the

THE CLERGY: A KEY ELEMENT

tribal populations, who were jealous of their independence, and for whom Shiism provided a religious idiom in which to give expression to their wish to keep the power of the Ottoman Empire at a distance.[2]

During the nineteenth century, the city of Najaf made itself the centre of Shia religious authority. From that time, it was in Najaf that the most powerful *ulama*, most of them of Iranian origin, would take up residence, and it was there that the most prestigious religious seminaries were established. The clerical institution in Iran had been structured around the exercise of functions granted by the state such as those of judges, administrators of religious bequests (*waqf*; plural form, *awqaf*), or *imams*.[3] In contrast, the clergy in Mesopotamia was organised around the activity of teaching. At that time, the influence of a cleric was measured primarily in terms of the number of students who attended his lessons. This is why the religious institution is referred to by the generic expression *hawza ilmiyya*, or "territory of knowledge".

The current predominance of Najaf over the other holy cities of Mesopotamia owes much to the skill of Mohammed Hasan Najafi (died 1849). As the most powerful religious leader of his day, he succeeded in building a far-reaching social network through the construction of a system of delegation of his authority to representatives, whom he deployed over a wide area to collect taxes and issue judgements in his name. This system meant he could impose his authority over the scholars of Mesopotamia's other holy cities and also over the wealthy merchants from Iran, who were the principal patrons of religious activities in Mesopotamia. He was thus able to lay down the earliest foundations of a religious administration based in Najaf. Najafi's successor, Murtadha Ansari (died 1864), consolidated his achievement by endowing it with a doctrinal foundation in the shape of the principle of the *marja'iyya al-taqlid*, literally the "imitation" of the most learned of the *ulama*. This lays down the principle that any Shia who has not mastered the ability to interpret the religious texts, the skill known as *ijtihad*, should follow the advice of a notably erudite scholar. This scholar would be known as the *marja' al-taqlid*, literally the "source of imitation", and would be designated by his peers following a highly informal procedure in which the social influence of the candidate was as significant as his religious erudition. Ideally, there should be only one *marja'*, whose authority should be agreed by consensus. In practice, however, a number of religious scholars have always disputed the monopoly of religious authority.

The establishment of the Iraqi state in 1921 ushered in a new era in the history of the Shia religious institution. In alliance with the tribal chiefs, the *ulama*, under the leadership of Mohammed Taqi al-Shirazi (died 1920), raised an army to drive the British out of Mesopotamia. Following the fall of the Ottoman Empire, the British had made themselves masters of the region, where they planned to create the new state of Iraq at whose head they planned to install their allies, the Hashemite dynasty of the Hijaz, one of whom was already on the throne of Transjordan (present-day Jordan). The Hashemite family were later finally expelled from the Hijaz by the Al Saud. A key episode in Iraqi history, the revolt led by the Shia *ulama*, is remembered by Iraqis as the revolution of 1920. The episode was to end, however, with a painful setback. Though the *ulama* inflicted substantial losses on the occupiers, they were in the end vanquished by the British army and lost their political power. Many *ulama* either chose to go into exile or were obliged to do so.

One consequence of the defeat of the *ulama* in Iraq was that Iran again attracted religious scholars. Najaf continued to be the site for the most prestigious seminaries, but those in Iran also underwent a resurgence. This was especially so for the city of Qom, where many of the exiles from Najaf took up residence. At the time, Qom was in essence a pilgrimage destination, as the site of the mausoleum of Fatima, the sister of the eighth Imam,

Ali al-Redha. It had been renowned in the past as a centre for religious studies, but its decline had set in with the mounting influence of the seminaries of Mesopotamia. The exile of the *ulama* of Najaf, however, led to its re-emergence as a religious centre of the first importance. The process was completed some decades later thanks to Iran's Islamic revolution in 1979, and because of the suppression of the seminaries in Iraq by the Baath (Resurrection) Party regime, with its Arab nationalist programme, which prompted a massive exodus of clerics from Iraq to Iran.

In terms of the scale of its infrastructure and the numbers of students, Qom is now incontestably the principal locality for the training of Shia clergy. During the years of oppression by the Baath dictatorship, the seminaries of Najaf were literally emptied, and the instability that has prevailed since the fall of Saddam Hussein has not so far allowed this process to be reversed. As the burial place of the Imam Ali, Najaf nevertheless retains a greater symbolic significance than that of Qom, and has continued to be the place of residence of the most important *maraji'* (the plural form of *marja'*). Thus, even during the period from 1979 to 1989 when Khomeini led the Islamic Republic and laid claim to the religious leadership of the Shia world, Abu al-Qasim al-Khoei (1899–1992), who exercised the *marja'iyya* from 1970 to 1992, and lived in Najaf despite his Iranian nationality, was incomparably more influential than Khomeini was. In short, though Qom became the scholarly centre of the Shia world, Najaf continued as the indisputable centre of religious authority.

The clergy and politics: Permanent revolution?

When the Islamic revolution in Iran took place, a debate began about the intrinsically revolutionary character of Shiism. Many pointed out that at the time Shia doctrine rested on concepts of political authority, which had led the Shias to reject all temporal power other than that of the Imam. The martyrdom at Karbala of the Third Imam, Hussein, is often taken as the key indication that the motive force of Shiism is intrinsically revolutionary. Hussein had decided to stand up to the Caliph Yazid in order to assert his right to reign. Abandoned at the last instant by his allies, he was aware that he and his family were destined for certain death but preferred nevertheless to make the sacrifice rather than submit to unjust rule.

This revolutionary interpretation of Hussein's death, however, is relatively recent, and has in essence been developed by the Shia Islamic movements. In Lebanon in the 1960s, under the influence of Musa al-Sadr and the Movement of the Deprived, the myth of Karbala was transformed from a ritual relating to fatalism and the acceptance of the established social order into a ritual of rebellion. Believers were exhorted no longer merely to weep tears of grief but instead to follow Hussein's example in fighting against the injustice of the established order without fear of sacrifice. At the same time, in Iran, the writings of Ali Shariati (1933–1977), called for a return to an original Shiism free of the interpretations of the *ulama*, within which the martyrdom of Hussein would serve as the model for political action. This style of interpretation would lie at the heart of the discourse employed during the Islamic revolution.

In reality, however, though the myth of Karbala has been reinterpreted for the modern age, this is precisely because the Shias experienced it in the past purely as a ritual of repentance for the collective failure of the Shia community, without prospect of changing the established historic order. In practice, the Shias themselves portray their doctrine and their history as informed by two contradictory tendencies, symbolised by the life choices of the second and third Imams: Hassan and Hussein. Hassan, the brother and predecessor of Hussein, chose peaceful coexistence with the Caliph and agreed to covet no more than the sta-

THE CLERGY: A KEY ELEMENT

tus of religious leader. The majority of his successors would choose the same course.

In the West, the opposition between Hassan and Hussein has often been identified with opposition between quietist and revolutionary courses of action, and it has been pointed out, with some justice, that the quietist tendency has historically prevailed over that which favours revolution, even in the period after the Iranian revolution. It is in the light of this perspective that some have sought to justify the American intervention in Iraq, emphasising that the rise to power of the Shias in Baghdad has enabled the quietist tendency represented by Ali al-Sistani (born 1930) to gain in prominence at the expense of the radical Ayatollahs of Qom. The reality, however, indicates the limitations of such a dualistic approach which seeks to divide the Shia clergy into revolutionaries and quietists. In the immediate aftermath of the fall of Saddam Hussein, the prominent political role played by Ali-al-Sistani, the most followed *marja'* in the Shia world and the leader of the *hawza* of Najaf since 1992, indicated that he regarded the adoption of a political stance as an integral part of his role as a religious leader. It was clear that he did not think that the *ulama* should attempt to take upon themselves the political powers of the Imam. Nevertheless, in common with the vast majority of his peers, he considered that it was obligatory for religious scholars to take a stand on the great issues of the day, especially in the event of serious political crisis. If he had abstained hitherto from taking up such a position, this was only because the circumstances that prevailed under the dictatorship of Saddam Hussein obliged him do to so. In taking on a high profile political role, he was in practice in sympathy with the predominant ideas of the clergy. His role, as he saw it, was to enunciate broad rules and resolve conflicts, and by doing so to ensure that the religious institution continued to be an essential actor in the political arena and in social life in general.

Historical precedents were numerous, including the revolution of 1920 in Iraq for example. Towards the end of the 1950s in

Iraq, the *hawza* of Najaf, under the influence of the *marja'* of the day, Muhsin al-Hakim (died 1970), organised itself once more to combat the influence of the secular ideologies promoted by successive Iraqi regimes. In Iran, the clergy was also at the centre of the debates on constitutional issues during the revolution of 1905–1911, when it was split equally between supporters and opponents of the democratic regime. In neither case did the clergy seek to govern the state directly. Rather, it agreed to coexist with the temporal authorities to the extent that these recognised the central role of religion and the religious institution in society.

Shia Political Islam at the heart of the clerical institution in Iraq

In Iraq, political Shiism first came into existence within the clerical institution of the country's holy cities. Here it was deeply influenced by the clerical institution's ideas, as well as by the institution's organisation and its internal quarrels. The first Shia political party, al-Da'wa al-Islamiyya ("The Islamic Call"), came into being in 1957–1958 in Najaf, within a clergy that was in crisis. The mounting secularisation of society was making itself felt through the rise of Arab nationalism and communism. The Shias, and in particular the new middle classes and those of more modest means, were attracted by these movements, which represented a challenge to the monarchy that the British had installed. Large numbers joined the Communist Party, which, it was said, played on the resonance between the Arabic words *shuyu'i* (communist) and *shi'i* (Shia) when recruiting in Shia circles.

However, for a movement that depended exclusively on the voluntary contributions of the faithful, secularisation had immediate consequences in terms of the ability of the Shia establishment to maintain itself. The fall of the monarchy following the coup mounted by General Abd al-Karim Qasim, with the sup-

THE CLERGY: A KEY ELEMENT

port of the Communists, came as a warning to the clergy, who realised that they needed to throw off their lethargy in order to regain some part of their former clientele. The situation became more serious with the promulgation of laws by Iraq's new leader that directly threatened the interests of the clergy. These included a new family law, which deprived the clergy of much of its judicial privilege, and also a new agrarian law that would over time eliminate the class of great landowners, who had traditionally financed clerical institutions.

While the initiative came originally from the middle and lower ranks of the clergy, political Shiism was also supported by the *marja'iyya*. Muhsin al-Hakim, who was at the time the master of Najaf, declared that the communist militants were not Muslims. With the support of the Association of Ulama, which he set up in 1960, he began to publish tracts written in language accessible to the less literate in which he rebutted communist doctrine and explained that Islam provided the most efficacious solutions to contemporary social problems. At the same time, he developed a network of religious schools and libraries intended to spread Islamic ideas. Though Muhsin al-Hakim was never formally a member of al-Da'wa, his closest students and his own son, Mahdi al-Hakim, were among the party's founders.

The most significant figure within al-Da'wa was undoubtedly Mohammed Baqir al-Sadr (1935–1980). It was he who wrote the party's constitution and developed its programme, taking the Muslim Brotherhood as his direct inspiration and producing a Shia version of the ideas of the Sunni movement that had come into being in Egypt in 1928, some thirty years before. As one of Muhsin al-Hakim's most brilliant students, he distinguished himself not only by his militant activity but also through his contributions to contemporary Islamic thought, which refuted communism point by point while proposing in its place a comprehensive Islamic system. Some of his formulations directly inspired those who drafted the first constitution for the Islamic republic in Iran in 1979, despite Mohammed Baqir al-Sadr having envisaged the religious scholars as counsellors rather than in the governmental role that they took in Iran.

The relationship of the clergy to the Da'wa party is indicative of the manner in which the Shia *ulama* understood their connection with politics. The creation of the party was itself a clear demonstration of the clergy's acceptance of the principle of a religious political party. As will be seen, however, such an outcome was not to come to pass without clashes and contradictions. At the same time, though the central concern of the clergy was the survival of the religious institution itself, and this would always take precedence over its political commitment. Muhsin al-Hakim's sincere view was that the establishment of a political party could make a contribution to the reinforcement of the *hawza*. In 1960, however, when he felt that militant activity risked of destabilising the *hawza*, he instructed Mohammed Baqir al-Sadr, as well as his own son, Mahdi al-Hakim, to resign from al-Da'wa. In short, as the clergy saw it, politics was often to be seen not as an end in itself, but as a means to shore up the religious institution. This was to become in due course a major point of contention with the non-clerical militants in the Islamic parties.

Factional quarrels

The institution of the *marja'iyya*, the supreme religious authority, is periodically convulsed by clashes between *ulama* who are candidates for the status of *marja'*. There are no explicit rules governing the appointment of *maraji'*, where candidates stake their claim over time through the mobilisation of their social networks. This lies at the origin of a situation where the authority of one *marja'* may be called into question by another who claims to be more learned or more modern in his approach to Islam. Such quarrels are often superimposed on regional or ethnic specificities.

THE CLERGY: A KEY ELEMENT

In the mid 1960s, a new Shia Islamic movement came into existence in Iraq as a result of the resurgence of the old rivalry between the cities of Najaf and Karbala. Before Najaf established itself as the principal centre of religious authority, it was at Karbala that the most important religious leaders had been based. In the mid-nineteenth century, following an abortive rising against the Ottoman government, Karbala was besieged and thousands of its inhabitants were massacred, leading to an exodus of *ulama* to Najaf and the decline of Karbala's seminaries. The scholars of Karbala, however, never entirely accepted their eclipse. In 1960, a young religious scholar named Mohammed al-Shirazi (1926–2001), whose father had run the main religious seminary in Karbala, declared himself to be a *marja'* and inaugurated an energetic campaign—described by his detractors as "aggressive"—to impose himself as a religious authority. Then as now, the *marja'iyya* was a gerontocratic institution where only men in their seventies were seen as legitimate candidates. At the age of thirty-four, Mohammed al-Shirazi was immediately categorised by the establishment in Najaf as an upstart, particularly because he had been little seen at the seminaries of Najaf, while he asserted that those in Karbala were as good if not better.

Al-Shirazi's campaign was conducted on various levels. On the one hand, he brought his family connections strongly into play. He was, as it happened, the scion of a prestigious line of *ulama* which had included several *maraji'*, including the renowned Mirza Hassan Shirazi (died 1894) who had in 1891 compelled the Shah to withdraw the monopoly over the tobacco trade in Iran that he had granted to the British. Another of his kin was the equally celebrated Mohammed Taqi Shirazi, who had led the 1920 revolution in Iraq. On the other hand, he also played on the sentiment of local belonging of the inhabitants of Karbala, who sought to promote the reputation and influence of their city in the face of what was seen as Najaf's arrogance. In addition, he presented himself as a reformer of the religious institution, which he wished to see more involved in worldly affairs and more politically active. Turning away from the jargon and abstruse language of the *ulama*, he issued many publications appealing to a popular audience.

Like Mohammed Baqir al-Sadr, Mohammed al-Shirazi took the view that the best method of combating secularisation was to fight on the terrain of politics. In his view, the clergy should not merely be the spearhead of mobilisation but should also be at the heart of the political machinery of the state. Anticipating Khomeini, he formulated a doctrine proposing government of the state by the clergy, a system he later categorised as *shurat al-fuqaha* (the council of the scholars). The Islamic state, in his view, should be governed by a collegiate institution that would bring together all the *maraji'*. By the same token, while he favoured the establishment of a fully political movement, he judged that it should be put directly under the control of the *marja'iyya*. He spoke out against al-Da'wa, which was, in his view, a Western-style political party, autonomous from the supreme religious authority, which was thus liable at any moment to veer off in some direction not sanctioned by Islam. His brother, Hassan al-Shirazi (1934–1980) dwelt particularly on this point in his writings, which directly inspired the nephew of the two Shirazi brothers, Mohammed Taqi al-Mudarrisi (born 1945). In the mid-1960s, Mudarrisi established a movement initially known as the Message Movement, which after 1979 took the title by which it is known to this day: the Islamic Action Organisation (*Munazzamat al-'Amal al-Islami*). Due to the strength of family links within the organisation, which was centred on the Shirazi family together with a handful of other clerical and merchant families in Karbala linked to it by marriage, the network that took shape around Mohammed al-Shirazi is familiarly known as that of the "Shirazists".

THE CLERGY: A KEY ELEMENT

The Iranian clergy and the state

In contrast to the clergy of Iraq, the clergy in Iran had always been hand in glove with the state. It was for this reason that they were especially distressed by the modernist reforms undertaken by the Pahlavi dynasty, which reigned from 1925 to 1979. In the first instance, the reform of the educational system, with the resulting expansion in the number of schools and civil establishments where priority was given to non-religious issues, put an end to the monopoly of the *ulama* over teaching. Then, the reform of the judicial system, with the introduction of civil courts, soon to be followed by the complete abolition of the religious tribunals, took away their judicial privileges. At the same time, the Shah initiated an extension of state control over the *hawza*, so that henceforth the government would have a voice in the curriculum of the religious seminaries. Through the creation of a faculty of theology at the University of Teheran, he also set up an alternative system for the training of clergy in competition with the traditional *hawza*. At the same time, there was an authoritarian secularisation of popular customs, with the obligatory westernisation of dress, for example, and its corollary of a ban on the headscarf for women, amongst other consequences. Lastly it should be noted that in the field of politics the clergy was faced by the emergence of left-wing movements, such as the Tudeh, the Iranian communist party, and Mohammed Mosaddeq's National Front, which acquired a monopoly over organised opposition against the Shah and left the clergy little room for manoeuvre in this area.

As had been the case in Iraq, the consequence of the crisis in the religious institution in Iran, from the 1940s onwards, was the re-politicisation of the Iranian clergy, after the religious institution grasped that it must take action, even if only to ensure its own survival. In practice, the movement inaugurated by Khomeini in 1963 was only one stage in a broader process, and his initiative was in any case belated in relation to those of other religious scholars. The example of Abu al-Qasim Kashani (1882–1962) deserves mention. He was educated in Najaf and took part in the 1920 revolution in Iraq, after which, like many others, he went into exile in Qom. Under the Soviet and British occupation of Iran in 1941, he involved himself once more in political activism and became a central figure. From 1951 to 1953, while the nationalist movement headed by Mohammed Mosaddeq was in power, he served as the speaker of parliament, representing the religious wing of Mosaddeq's movement. Kashani was also linked to an Islamic movement, the Devotees of Islam (*Fada'iyan e-Islam*), which was founded in 1945 by a group of clerics led by Navvab Safavi (1924–1955). Like al-Da'wa in Iraq, this movement took its inspiration from the ideas of the Muslim Brotherhood.

As regards Khomeini, it was only in the 1960s that he entered the political arena, so that he can in some respects be considered before this to have been more typical of the quietist Ayatollahs, though with the reservations that have already been attached to the use of this expression. More concerned with his own career in the religious institution than with fulmination against the policies of the Shah, he held himself scrupulously aloof from the political crises of the 1950s. Thus, he collaborated closely with Mohammed Burujerdi (died 1961), who at the time the was leading *marja'* and took a deeply hostile line to such activist clerics as Kashani. When Burujerdi passed away, Khomeini declared his own *marja'iyya*, despite there being other *ulama* regarded at the time as more learned. When Khomeini entered the political fray in 1963, with a celebrated speech against the Shah, he lagged yet again behind others. By the time he was arrested, having led a demonstration against laws on the emancipation of women and agrarian reform, and against the agreement to borrow American money to buy arms, the *hawza* at Qom had already been mobilised weeks before.

The consequences for Khomeini, however, are widely known. Given the pressure he was under, the holy cities in Iraq naturally presented themselves as the best refuge. From 1964, he lived in exile in Najaf, until his expulsion by the Iraqi regime in 1978, after which he fled to France before returning in triumph to Iran in 1979 to take up the reins of power. It was during his sojourn in Najaf that his political ideas developed further and that he formulated the theory of the *wilayat al-faqih*, the government of the state by the most learned of the *ulama*, that is to say, by the *marja'*.

Up to the present day, the details of Khomeini's stay in Najaf are unclear. It appears that he was relatively isolated from the religious institution, including the militants of al-Da'wa, who eventually found themselves embarrassed as to how to relate to him. Undoubtedly, their political ideas were close to his, but both the Da'wa party and the *marja'iyya* of Najaf had taken up an ambiguous stance in relation to the regime of the Shah. Their philosophy was antagonistic to the authoritarian modernisation espoused by the Pahlavis, and they were clearly opposed to the suppression of the seminaries of Qom. However, they must have been aware that the Shah was providing them with practical and political support. In the context of the still latent rivalry between Iran and Iraq, al-Da'wa provided the Shah with an invaluable instrument for the destabilisation of the Iraqi regime. The Shah also supported Muhsin al-Hakim against the Ayatollahs of Qom, in order to undermine the Iranian clergy, and forestall their development as a powerful opposition force. In this context, Khomeini was actually an embarrassing guest for the *hawza* of Najaf, as it was felt that any overt sympathy for him might alienate the Shah, whose support was so important.

At the time, only the Shirazists, who condemned the Shah's demands without reservation, gave their backing to Khomeini's struggle. In addition to such symbolic actions as the organisation of a formal ceremony of welcome for Khomeini when he arrived in Iraq, the Shirazists also provided practical help to him and to his supporters; they provided his associates with counterfeit passports, for example. In return, the Khomeinists helped the Shirazists, both before and after the revolution. For example, it was through the intervention of Khomeini's supporters that the Shirazists were given military training in the camps run in Lebanon by the PLO (the Palestine Liberation Organisation) in the 1970s. The Palestinians supported the opposition to the Shah because his regime was Israel's principal regional ally. In contrast, they withheld their support from movements that opposed the existing Arab regimes, since the material and political assistance furnished to the Palestinians by these regimes was indispensable. It was therefore only by passing themselves off as Iranians of Arab ethnicity from the Iranian frontier region of Khuzistan, where there was a substantial Arab minority, that the Iraqi Shirazists, with the connivance of Khomeini's associates, were able to benefit from the Palestinians' military expertise. After the Iranian revolution, this privileged relationship, built up over a period of fifteen years, put the Shirazists in a position where they were able to exercise a determining influence over the politics of exporting the Iranian revolution to the region, particularly in the countries of the Gulf.

Clergy and laity: A *"structuring cleavage"*

While the clergy has played a prominent part within the various Shia Islamic movements, and to a considerable extent is still important in them, these movements have also always included laymen. It can even be said that the ideological split between laity and clergy, sometimes even taking the form of real antagonism between these two groups, is a "structuring cleavage": a dichotomy that constitutes an intrinsic feature of the structure of Shia political Islam. It was in Iran that this dichotomy was initially most marked, in particular as exemplified in the figure of Ali Shariati. At a time when Khomeini had not yet made his entry into politics, Shariati was a supporter of Mossadeq's

THE CLERGY: A KEY ELEMENT

nationalist movement. Shariati was a brilliant student of the humanities and had gone to Paris in the early 1960s to work on a thesis at the Sorbonne. The years he spent in France were critical to his intellectual development. He discovered the philosophy of Jean-Paul Sartre and the sociology of Georges Gurvitch, as well as the anti-colonialist literature of Franz Fanon. He also sought out the orientalists, such as Jacques Berque and Louis Massignon, and the militants of the Algerian liberation movement. Reconciling the apparently very different approaches of one group and another, he constructed over time a religious ideology maintaining that a return to Islam was the only real solution to the socio-political problems facing the Shias.

Meanwhile, Ali Shariati's conception of Islam set him apart from the religious and political conceptions of the *ulama*, even of the most politically aware among them. His vision for Islam, for which he was bitterly reproached, was very close to that of the Sunni faith, with its advocacy of the suppression of all forms of mediation between God and the faithful, and especially of the intervention of the clergy. He contrasted his idea of an original and pure Shiism, that of Imam Ali, with the institutionalised and corrupt Shiism of the Safavids, of which the contemporary religious institution was, as he saw it, the direct descendant. Like the Sunni Islamic activists he called for a return to a purified Islam liberated from the blemishes that had resulted from interpretation by the *ulama*. His position could not fail to arouse the hostility of the Iranian clergy, including the reformists and revolutionaries who would later gravitate towards the entourage of Ayatollah Khomeini, such as Morteza Mottahari (died 1979). However, while regarding Shariati's ideas as dangerous, this group also took the view that such ideas could make a contribution towards bringing the younger generation back to the correct path of Islam. Mottahari therefore agreed to allow Shariati to join the Ershad (Guidance) Institute which he had established for the propagation of Islamic thought. In the 1970s, Shariati was one of the Institute's most popular lecturers, which made the government and the *ulama* uneasy. Even within the management committee of the Institute itself, his presence was a source of regular clashes between clerics and laymen.

Far from being an isolated case, the experience of Ali Shariati was indicative of a broader social phenomenon relating to the emergence of those who became known as "religious modernists". These were a category of learned men who had not studied in the religious seminaries, but had been trained in secular disciplines, often in the sciences, who were nevertheless also able to display legitimate religious scholarship, which they put to political ends.[4] In Iran, this phenomenon found expression through the Movement for the Liberation of Iran (MLI) particularly. This movement was established in 1961 by religious intellectuals and a group of reformist clerics, some of whom would later be centrally involved in the 1979 revolution and who occupied key posts in the months after the fall of the Shah. They included Mehdi Bazargan (1907–1995), the first head of the Iranian government after the revolution, and Sadeq Gotbzadeh (1936–1981), who was briefly minister of Foreign Affairs but was executed in 1981 for having plotted to overthrow Khomeini. Other members were Mostafa Chamran (1932–1981), Minister of Defence and head of the Pasdaran[5] until his death in the Iran-Iraq war, and Mahmud Taleqani (1912–1979), one of the few clerics in the movement, who died only a few months after the revolution.

The MLI was opposed to the Shah's policy of authoritarian modernisation and agitated for the introduction of a democracy that would fully embody religious values. Though the movement participated in the Islamic Revolution and afterwards became a part of the institutions of the new regime, it never accepted the *wilayat al-faqih*, the principle of government by the clergy as conceived by Khomeini. The activists of the MLI were much less anti-clerical than Ali Shariati, who was for a time one of its

THE CLERGY: A KEY ELEMENT

members. They considered that the *ulama* had a key role to play in political change but that they should nevertheless not be installed as the supreme political authority. It is significant that, after the clergy had consolidated its grip on the Islamic Republic, the MLI became an opposition movement. This indicated that coexistence between the religious modernists and the clergy was not easy.

Though it was in Iran that the phenomenon of religious modernism achieved its most developed form, it was not restricted to that country. To a greater or lesser extent, all the Shia Islamic movements, in whatever country they might be situated, were drawn from the same category of lay activists who strove to bring about a society in which religious values would be central, while at the same time refusing to entrust the power of political decision-making to the clergy. In Iraq and in the Gulf monarchies, such people are colloquially known as *effendi*. This was an expression whose use was revealing in itself, since it originated in Ottoman times as a word that in the Arab world became an honorific title attached to a highly westernised urban and literate class rather than to members of the clergy.[6] Such persons were mainly educated in modern institutions based on the western model and free from the traditional oversight of the religious authorities. An indication of their particular background was that they adopted a style of dress that mingled traditional Ottoman characteristics with the contemporary western mode. They wore a three piece suit together with a tarboush. This form of headgear, a truncated cone of dark red fabric with a flat top adorned by a black silk tassel, was widespread in the nineteenth century Ottoman Empire.

The contemporary use of the word *effendi* by the Shia Islamic activists echoes perfectly its former use. It refers to those activists, mainly graduates in lay subjects (such as engineering, medicine and law) whose religious culture is both self-taught and derived from contact with discussion groups more or less directly linked with the religious institution. It is not unusual to find amongst such *effendis* former militants from Marxist and nationalist movements. These often explain that their belated adherence to whichever religious movement they have joined is not due to a lack of faith but to their initial scepticism regarding the religious institution. Only when clerics who had broken with the classical model made their appearance, such as Mohammed Baqir al-Sadr, Ruhollah Khomeini, Musa al-Sadr, Mohammed al-Shirazi, did they revise their ideological attachments. Nevertheless, as will be seen, their antipathy towards the clergy has remained for the most part unchanged.

2

TRANSNATIONAL NETWORKS

The concentration of religious authority in Najaf established it as the centre of Shiism, while the remainder of the Shia world is on the periphery. Before this, religious authority had for the most part been exercised on a strictly local level, covering only a particular town or region. Centralisation eventually meant that the seminaries of Najaf became an obligatory rite of passage for any cleric ambitious to play any significant social role. In general, once a cleric's training was complete, he returned to his country armed with certificates from his teachers attesting to his level of competence together with a written authorisation from the *marja'iyya* to collect taxes or set up an educational establishment in its name. In short, the authority of a Lebanese or Saudi scholar was dependent on his closeness to Najaf, that is to say, in practical terms, to the degree to which he was part of a network of relationships that linked him directly to the supreme religious authority. The centralisation of religious authority in Najaf had therefore the effect of bringing into existence a transnational clerical infrastructure spanning the Shia world. From the close of the 1960s, this has been a key element in the system of recruitment of Shia Islamic activists and their movement from one place to another. It is what perpetuates the interconnection between Shia movements across the Middle East.

Al-Da'wa on the national and transnational plane

Many of the clerical activists in Middle Eastern Shia Islamic movements were trained in Najaf in the 1960s and 1970s, the period when al-Da'wa was playing a central role in the re-politicisation of the clergy and was especially influential amongst religious students. Al-Da'wa has always been torn between two concepts of political action. On the one hand, it was an Iraqi party whose scope was limited to the territory of that country, within which its goal was the overthrow of the regime and its replacement by an Islamic state. This view was particularly that of the *effendis* (the lay activists). On the other hand, al-Da'wa was also seen by many as a preaching movement whose vocation was the dissemination of Islam far beyond the frontiers of Iraq. This conception was that of the *ulama*, in particular, for whom political action could only have meaning in relation to the whole community of believers, the *umma*. Though the principal objective of al-Da'wa was certainly to overthrow established governments, Iraq was seen in practice as only the initial step of a process that must in due course come to include the whole of the *dar al-islam*, the territory of the Muslims, considered as the only legitimate territorial boundary. For such clerics, Iraq, in common with other Middle Eastern states, was not a legitimate political entity, since it had been created by the colonial powers and had divided the Muslims. In reality, religion rather than nationality was the sole relevant division within society. Ideally, therefore, the sovereignty of an Islamic state should reach far beyond the frontiers of nation states. For the same reason, al-Da'wa should recruit more widely than among Iraqis alone. In practice, while the majority of al-Da'wa militants were Iraqis, the party included non-Iraqis and had drawn into its political ambit Shia figures in Lebanon, Bahrain, Kuwait and the United Arab Emirates (UAE).

The Najaf connection in Lebanon and Bahrain

In Lebanon, two eminent figures from the Lebanese religious scene were drawn into the circle of al-Daʿwa, namely Mohammed Hussein Fadlallah (1935–2010) and Mohammed Mahdi Shams al-Din (1936–2001). Mohammed Hussein Fadlallah, closely associated with the Hezbollah movement, was born in Najaf into a family of clerics originating from Jabal Amil in southern Lebanon, and since 1995 had been one of the most followed *marajiʿ* in the Shia world. Meanwhile, between 1978 and 2001 Mohammed Mahdi Shams al-Din had been the head of the Shia Higher Islamic Council, the institution that represents the Shiite community in Lebanon. He is also well known for his philosophical writings.

The relationship of Fadlallah and Shams al-Din with al-Daʿwa had always been ambiguous, with both men denying they were in any way affiliated to the party. It is true that neither had occupied any visible position in the command structure of al-Daʿwa in Iraq. On the one hand, it remains open to question whether either had at any time been officially a member, and there is not enough reliable information to form a definitive answer.[1] On the other hand, what is certain is that during their time in Iraq both were members in good standing of the Association of Ulama of Najaf, an organisation established in 1960 by Muhsin al-Hakim in order to re-Islamise society through the publication of tracts and magazines disseminated through a chain of libraries and Islamic schools. Links between al-Daʿwa and the Association were close, and the publisher of the Association's journal, "Lights" (*Al-Adwaʾ*), was Mohammed Baqir al-Sadr. In fact, Fadlallah and Shams al-Din's refusal to openly acknowledge their links with al-Daʿwa, or indeed to acknowledge publicly any allegiance of a party political nature, should be seen in the context of the customary discretion of high-ranking clerics in their dealings with political parties. Clerics who support political parties and share their ideological position often maintain their distance to avoid undermining their position within the religious institution. They might otherwise appear to be in a position to be utilised by groups whose objectives, and in particular whose methods, are far from being unanimously approved by the *hawza*.

However, there is some consensus that when Fadlallah returned from Najaf at the end of the 1960s, he started up a branch of al-Da'wa in Lebanon. Nevertheless, the movement remained underground and, rather than acting independently, its method of operation was instead to infiltrate other existing organisations in order to influence them from within. In this manner, many al-Da'wa militants became members of the Movement of the Deprived, set up by Musa al-Sadr in 1973 and of Hezbollah when it was formed in 1982, into which al-Da'wa was finally merged. Amongst these were, for instance, Subhi al-Tufayli (born 1948), who was secretary-general of Hezbollah in the 1980s, and Naim Qasim (born 1952), the deputy secretary-general of Hezbollah at the time of writing.

Ali al-Kurani (born 1944) is a figure less known to the public, but who nevertheless played a more important role in al-Da'wa than did either Fadlallah or Shams al-Din. Also a native of Jabal Amil in Lebanon, he occupied a central position in the command structure of the party and took a key part in its dissemination beyond the frontiers of Iraq: in Lebanon and especially in Kuwait. In the early 1980s, Kurani had been responsible, with others, for one of the earliest schisms within al-Da'wa. At that time, he joined with a faction of militants from the southern Iraqi city of Basra to challenge the system by which party officials were elected. The group demanded that posts be allotted to individuals according to the amount of party activity they had undertaken. Finding themselves in the minority, the challengers set up a splinter group, al-Da'wa al-Islamiyya (Basra Line), which Kurani was, however, soon to leave. His career was especially revealing in terms of the tension between the national and the transnational dimensions of al-Da'wa. In one sense, his presence within the command structure showed that a non-Iraqi origin was no bar to the achievement of responsibility within the party. On the other hand, the dissident movement in which he participated indicated that the Iraqis, and those from Najaf in particular, were still on top. In addition, over the years, as will be seen, al-Da'wa became an exclusively Iraqi national party. The secession by the Basra Line can clearly be interpreted in this light. Militants from southern Iraq, and more generally all those not identified with political and religious centre represented by Najaf, rejected the principle of election in a move to overcome the local partialities that would certainly predominate in any electoral process.

The establishment of al-Da'wa in Bahrain provides another instance of the way traditional relationships of religious authority influenced the way that the party spread across national frontiers. Here, it was Bahraini students drawn into the political ambit of al-Da'wa during their stay in Najaf who spread the party's ideology after their return to their own country at the end of their training and set up local affiliates. Some joined the party directly in Iraq, including Suleiman al-Madani (1939–2003) and his brother Abdallah al-Madani (1939–1976). These two were students at Najaf in the 1960s and participated in 1968 in the foundation of the Islamic Enlightenment Society (*Jama'iyyat al-Tawu'iyya al-Islamiyya*) which was to become the front organisation for al-Da'wa in Bahrain, a country where political parties were at the time banned. Both were persuaded to go over to the government side and promptly left the party. Suleiman accepted a position as a religious judge and in 1997 was appointed head of the Sharia Appeal Court, becoming in due course the leader of those Shia Islamic activists who supported the regime. Abdallah was murdered in 1976 by militant Marxists, who regarded him as a tool of the government against the parties of the left, which at the time led the opposition. In the early 1970s, the emergence of religious movements was seen at first by the Bahraini government, as it was by other regimes, as an opportunity to counterbalance the so-called "progressive" movements of Marxist or Arab Nationalist sympathy, or both. Only at a later time did they constitute an opposition force.

In Bahrain, everything changed with the crisis of 1975. In 1973, a number of al-Da'wa militants were elected to the first parliament in the country's history, where they became in numerical terms the second parliamentary group after that formed by the progressives. When the government attempted to introduce an emergency law in 1974 without seeking parliamentary approval, the al-Da'wa group finally decided to throw in their lot with their political adversaries in rejecting any compromise. In 1975, the regime dissolved the assembly, plunging the country into a political crisis that has never since been truly resolved.

In Bahrain today, most of the leading opposition figures, whose recurrent preoccupation is the re-establishment of parliament and the constitution which they voted for in 1973, emerged from al-Da'wa and were also members, often in responsible positions, of the Islamic Enlightenment Society. A particular case is that of Isa Qasim (born 1943), who has been since 2001 by far the most influential cleric on the Shia political and religious scene. Educated in Najaf in the 1960s, his political career began in 1972 when he returned to Bahrain to take part in the parliamentary elections. He was elected by an overwhelming majority in his constituency, after which he became the head of the Islamic Enlightenment Society. Since 2004, he has also been the head of the Islamic Council of Ulama, whose brief is to maintain the independence of the Shia religious institution from the government. Today, however, Isa Qasim is best known as the spiritual leader of al-Wifaq ("The Accord"), the largest political party in the country, which has since 2001 included all the factions of the Shia Islamic opposition. Though he has no formal link with al-Wifaq, he is nevertheless seen as wielding moral authority over its controlling institutions, though his practical power must not be overestimated, this book will show. Nevertheless, his endorsement is a significant element of al-Wifaq's legitimacy, in the population's eyes and those of the religious institution.

In addition to Isa Qasim, others with similar careers have recently played a central part in politics. One such is Abdallah al-Ghurayfi (born 1944). He is a member of a major clerical family which has branches in both Iran and Iraq.[2] During the years of his education in Najaf, he maintained a personal relationship with Mohammed Baqir al-Sadr that is described as "close" by many in Bahrain. He was part of the entourage of Mohammed Hussein Fadlallah until the latter's death in 2010, having in the 1990s managed Fadlallah's *hawza* at Sayyida Zaynab in Syria. The two men were therefore very close, to the extent that Ghurayfi pronounced Fadlallah's funeral oration and was often mentioned by Bahrainis as Fadlallah's successor and thus potentially the first Bahraini *marja'* for decades. Though his influence in Bahrain was less than that of Isa Qasim, he was recognised as al-Wifaq's alternative patron and made regular pronouncements on Bahraini politics. A further figure without whom the list of personalities drawn into al-Da'wa in the 1970s would not be complete was Abd al-Amir al-Jamri (born 1937), who died after a long illness in 2006. Jamri was at the heart of what was known as the *intifada*, the popular uprising which destabilised the Bahraini regime between 1994 and 1999, which led to his epithet of the "fighting sheikh".[3]

The marja'iyya and the merchant notability of the Gulf

The organisation of the clergy is only one aspect of the process of transnationalisation of al-Da'wa, which also depends on the nature of the relationship between the *marja'iyya* and local society, and, even more, on the personalities it has as its interlocutors. In practice, much depends on the degree of "clericalisation" of society, or in other words on the scale of the local religious institution and its role in social life. Thus, societies such as Lebanon, Bahrain and Saudi Arabia, which have a long-standing, well-organised and influential religious class, must be distinguished from such societies as Kuwait, the United Arab Emirates and Oman. In these latter countries, the clergy has put down only shallow roots and its social influence is sharply curtailed by that of the class of merchant notables. The economic power of this latter group can be very significant, for example in Dubai and Oman, and is reflected in the central role it plays in religious life. In contrast to the clergy, whose field of action consists in essence of teaching and jurisdiction in matters of family law, the notables play a role in the organisation of popular religion. For the most part, it is they who finance the construction of mosques and of *husseiniyyat* (singular form, *husseiniyya*: these are Shia places of worship associated with the mourning of the martyred Imam Hussein), often named after their founders. They also organise the commemorative rituals for the births and deaths of the "Fourteen Infallibles", as the twelve Imams together with the Prophet Mohammed and his daughter Fatima are known. Their role is particularly important during Ashura, the celebration that commemorates the martyrdom of Imam Hussein.

This low level of clerical influence itself reflects a particular variety of socio-historical evolution. By comparison with Lebanon, Bahrain and Saudi Arabia, Shiism has arrived relatively recently in Kuwait, the United Arab Emirates and Oman. It is the result of successive waves of migration from the mid-eighteenth century to the first half of the twentieth century, from Iran and Bahrain, as well as from Hasa (a province of eastern Saudi Arabia) and from Sind (Pakistan's coastal province). The reasons for this migration were very diverse. Some came as traders or simply to seek work in countries where there was an economic boom with the rise of overseas trade, first with the advent of pearl diving and then, from the 1940s, the petroleum industry. Others sought refuge from religious persecution. This was especially the case for the Shias of Bahrain and Saudi Arabia after the conquest of most of the Arabian Peninsula by Sunni tribes from the central region of Nejd in the eighteenth century. In the Bahrain archipelago, the Al Khalifa family, a Sunni dynasty still in power today, took control of the arable land and the pearl fishing, subjecting the Shia peasants to a form of servitude that created a rift between the state and the Shia population which continues largely to account for current conflicts. In Saudi Arabia, the Al Saud legitimised their programme of conquest in terms of the propagation of "Wahhabism", a form of particularly rigorous Sunni orthodoxy inspired by the teachings of Mohammed ibn Abd al-Wahhab, positing the Shias as pagans that should be subjected by military force if necessary, if they could not be converted to the "true" religion.

Amongst the Shias who settled on the Arabian coast of the Gulf, only a few took up the religious vocation. The few religious scholars there were, for the most part, sent by the *marja'iyya* of Najaf at the request of some local merchant or other who had constructed a mosque and who, in order to enhance his social prestige, sought a properly trained cleric to officiate over the prayers and instruct the faithful. The *ulama* of Najaf often had to be begged to go to these distant lands, far from the principal centres of religious activity, which offered limited career prospects. Matters began to change, however, with the development of the petroleum industry, and even more with the oil price rise of 1973–74, which opened the way for rapid accumulation of wealth by the Shias of the Gulf. As the *marja'iyya* judged it, the Gulf emirates ceased at this point to be a backwater with an inhospitable climate and became a field for the propagation of Islam and for funds to be raised for their project of social re-conquest. Iraqi businessmen, who were frequently disinclined in any case to contribute to the works of the *ulama*, were unable to match the level of wealth of their opposite numbers in the Gulf and still fall short of that level. The local representatives of the *marja'iyya* in the oil monarchies therefore began to acquire a level of strategic importance they had not hitherto enjoyed, and were henceforth selected with particular care.

It is in this connection that the establishment of al-Da'wa in Kuwait must be viewed. In 1968, the al-Naqi family completed the construction of a mosque, contacting Muhsin al-Hakim's office to ask for the dispatch of a religious scholar of his choice to run it. The *marja'* sent Ali al-Kurani (see above), who was already an active member of al-Da'wa. Al-Kurani served as the principal representative of the *marja'iyya* in Kuwait for seven years, while a group of younger men gathered around him who aspired to break with the traditional forms of religious expression inherited from their parents. Fundamentally dissatisfied with the manner in which their coreligionists had been engaging with politics in Kuwait, these individuals believed Islam could be the catalyst for a new style of political action. Shia parliamentary representation at the time was dominated by merchant notables of Iranian origin. The notables in question maintained good relations with the ruling Al Sabah dynasty, whom they systematically supported against the opposition, and especially against the Arab nationalists, whose leaders were from the Sunni merchant oligarchy. The group of younger figures around Ali al-Kurani, however, took the view that the Shias had received scant reward for their loyalty. For instance, no Shia minister had ever been appointed. In addition, their numbers in parliament did not reflect their demographic importance, and could, as they saw it, be greater.

Amidst these young men desirous of change, there were a number of individuals who have become major figures in

Kuwaiti politics today. These include Adnan Abd al-Samad (born 1950), who is a member of the current legislature in Kuwait (elected in 2012) and was elected as a member of Kuwait's parliament on a total of seven previous occasions, as well as Abd al-Muhsin Jamal and Nasir Sarkhu, each elected three times. These men would meet at the al-Naqi mosque, where al-Kurani officiated, and later instituted a *diwaniyya*, a salon for the purpose of political discussion, which became known as the *Diwaniyya al-Shabab* (the young men's *diwaniyya*). This movement later became more formal when the "young men" took control of the Social Association for Culture (*Jama'iyya al-Thaqafa al-Ijtima'iyya*), at the election for its administrative council. This association had been established some years earlier by the Shia notables for the promotion of what was described as "Shia culture", which in practice consisted of the dissemination of diverse publications, including fiction and poetry, often with no direct link to religion but written by individuals socially identified as Shias. In 1972, the Association became the legally recognised front organisation for al-Da'wa in Kuwait, and served to advance the political ambitions of the "young men", of whom many entered parliament after the elections of 1981, thus dislodging the old guard of Shia notables once and for all from the political scene.

Suppression and exile

From the early 1970s onwards, another factor came into play in the reinforcement of the transnational networks of al-Da'wa in the Middle East: namely, the intensification of the suppression of Shia Islamic movements in Iraq. The climax came with the execution of Mohammed Baqir al-Sadr in 1980, which led to a large-scale exodus of militants. At this period, the old clerical networks served as an infrastructure facilitating the movement of the exiles and offering them protection. The exiles' status in the countries where they sought refuge was not always clear. Iran took in many exiles, if only because the Iraqi regime, prior to the Islamic revolution of 1979, had expelled Iraqis of Iranian origin en masse, and for the most part indiscriminately, in the belief that they were a Trojan horse for the Shah. Al-Da'wa activists were all the more welcome in Iran because the Shah, as has been seen, had long supported their party. The difficulty was that these exiles continued to be at the mercy of fluctuations in the bilateral relationship between Iran and Iraq. In 1975, for instance, after the Algiers agreement, aimed at resolving the frontier dispute, when relations between the two countries briefly improved, Mohammed Mahdi al-Asefi, a leading official of al-Da'wa who had fled to Iran, where members of his family were well viewed by the Shah, was obliged to leave the country for Kuwait. There, he succeeded Ali al-Kurani at the head of the al-Naqi mosque and continued his work of political outreach.

Just as his predecessor had done, he took care not to give the authorities the impression that he was a political exile. A constant demand of successive Iraqi regimes had been the annexation of Kuwait, which the Iraqis regarded as an integral part of their territory. Iraq had always supported the opposition to the Al Sabah dynasty so for Kuwait it was eminently logical to welcome Iraqi opposition figures. On the other hand, this was also a policy fraught with danger since Kuwait had little capacity to resist possible Iraqi reprisals. Kuwait therefore took in dozens of al-Da'wa officials, but on an unofficial footing and without permitting them to continue their political activities on Kuwaiti soil, which therefore remained clandestine. Their justification of staying in Kuwait lay in their relationship to the *marja'iyya*: they came to preserve the link between the Shia world's centre and its periphery, and, more generally, to disseminate their religious knowledge. Some of the Iraq al-Da'wa militants found posts in the National *Ja'fari*[4] School, at that time the only school that existed specifically for the education of Shias. One of these was the well-known al-Daʿwa exile Azz al-Din Salim (died 2004), who, together with Ali al-Kurani, had instigated the secession of the Basra faction (Basra being the city where he was originally from). In 2003, following the fall of Saddam Hussein, he joined the Interim Governing Council in Iraq and became its president in May 2004, which led to his assassination two weeks later in a car bomb attack.

The role of the Iraqi exiles in transnationalisation is also borne out by the experience of the United Arab Emirates, where a cell of al-Daʿwa, now dissolved, was established after the arrival in Dubai of Mahdi al-Hakim, the son of the *marjaʿ* Muhsin al-Hakim and founder of the party along with Mohammed Baqir al-Sadr. After being arrested and tortured in Iraq, he came to the UAE in 1971, where his activities had an impact on local Shia affairs. He helped obtain official recognition of the Shia presence in the country with his campaign for the creation of an administration for Shia *awqaf* (religious bequests; singular form *waqf*) in Dubai and Sharjah, the UAE's two principle centres of Shia population.[5] In 1980, Mahdi al-Hakim devolved his administrative functions to another member of al-Daʿwa, the Bahraini Abdallah al-Ghurayfi (see above) who remained in this post until the end of the 1980s.

The Shirazists: the other transnational network

The Shirazists also built up a transnational network in the course of the 1970s. Based in Karbala, they had set themselves up as the adversaries of the establishment in Najaf and as rivals to al-Daʿwa. Since they were at odds with the *marjaʿiyya* of Najaf, they were clearly not in a position to make use of Najaf's transnational infrastructure to facilitate their movements. It was, however, their overriding need to flee the territory of Iraq in order to escape from persecution that provided the impetus for their transnationalisation.

The first to go into exile, after months of torture in the Iraqi regime's prisons, was Hassan al-Shirazi. He based himself both in Lebanon and in Syria, where he continued his political activities and set up a number of religious teaching institutions. Only one of these still exists today: that based in Sayyida Zaynab on the outskirts of Damascus. This institution occupied a crucial position in the organisation of the Shirazist transnational network, especially in the 1990s. Today, it is still the largest Shia religious educational establishment in Syria. Though the Twelver Shia population of Syria is not large, amounting to only 0.5 per cent of the population, according to estimates, Syria has nevertheless increasingly attracted Shia refugees coming from Iraq, Afghanistan and the Gulf countries, especially Bahrain and Saudi Arabia. The Shirazists have played a key role in this process, after grasping early the opportunity presented to them by the little town of Sayyida Zaynab.

Situated just ten kilometres from Damascus, Sayyida Zaynab was scarcely more than a village in 1975 when Hassan al-Shirazi chose it as the location for his religious school. It was the site of the tomb of Zaynab, the sister of the Imam Hussein, who had been present at the battle of Karbala, where she distinguished herself by her courage. However, the building had long been allowed to fall into disrepair. It was restored at great expense by the Iranian regime in the 1990s, and today it is an impressive structure with a golden cupola and fine mosaics. Hassan al-Shirazi, however, saw that Sayyida Zaynab could have many advantages as the site of a clerical community. In the first instance, the premises were there for the taking, as no-one was interested in the site, and particularly not the *marja'iyya* of Najaf. In addition, the Syrian regime, for various reasons, had motives for supporting Shia religious activities. Not only could they serve as a weapon in the struggle with Iraq, in an era when Syria and Iraq were still ruled by rival branches of the Baath Party, but they could also be used as a tool for the legitimisation of the Syrian regime in the eyes of the population. Hafez al-Assad, then the president of Syria, was at the time the object of a challenge from the Sunni Islamic militants, who condemned his membership of a heterodox group, the Alawite sect, which had a loose link with Shiism. One element of his counter-attack was to court Shia clerics who were willing to recognise the relationship of the Alawite sect to Shiism and therefore to Islam.[6] Finally, Hassan-al-Shirazi's seminary, which he named the *Hawza Zaynabiyya*, fulfilled a real need, since the oppression of Shias in Iraq had led to the emigration of thousands of students and teachers, both Iraqis and foreigners. For many of these, the seminary of Sayyida Zaynab soon became an alternative *hawza*, whose significance in practical terms seemed destined only to increase.

The Gulf countries, and especially Kuwait, Bahrain, Saudi Arabia, and to a lesser extent Oman, would come to constitute the new redoubt for the Shirazists after their departure from Karbala. It was thanks to the financial support they found there that they were able to consolidate their position in the Shia religious and political landscape. Mohammed al-Shirazi settled in Kuwait in 1971 with his whole family: two of his brothers, his sisters, his sons and daughters and his mother, and also his nephews, of whom one was Mohammed Taqi al-Mudarrisi. Mohammed al-Shirazi had long thought of extending his support network into the Gulf countries, and even before taking up residence in Kuwait, he had kept a close eye on developments there. Karbala's position as a pilgrimage destination had enabled him to establish contact with many visitors from the Gulf states and a number of Kuwaiti merchants had made donations to his programme of activities. Through these contacts, he succeeded in establishing himself in Kuwait. He took up residence in the old Shia quarter of Bneid al-Gar, where, during the nine years of his stay, he set up a number of institutions that are still active today, including a religious seminary, a library, a mosque, a *huseiniyya* and a *diwaniyya*. In the 1990s, Saleh Ashur (born

1953), previously elected five times to the Kuwaiti legislature and once more a member of the current parliament, set up in Kuwait the offices of a large-scale charitable organisation, Ahl al-Bayt ("The Family of the Prophet", literally "The People of the House"). It raised funds to finance projects throughout the Shia world, from Iran and Azerbaijan to Pakistan. In the field of Kuwaiti politics, however, the Shirazists kept a relatively low profile. It was only in the 1990s, in the aftermath of the Gulf War of 1991 and the period of democratisation that followed, that they formed an organised political group, a member of which was elected to parliament in 1999. In terms of politics, Kuwait was a sanctuary that kept them safe while they took action in other regions, rather than a political objective in itself. A large proportion of the clerical officials of the various Shia Islamic movements in the Gulf that were linked to the Shirazi faction were trained in Kuwait, under the auspices of Mohammed Taqi al-Mudarrisi.

In fact, just as al-Da'wa had been transnationalised by the spreading influence of the *marja'iyya* of Najaf, the extension of Mohammed al-Shirazi's authority beyond Karbala led to the transnationalisation of the Message Movement (*Al-Haraka al-Risaliyya*, later known as the "Islamic Action Organisation"), set up by al-Mudarrisi in Iraq some years before. The interconnection between clerical and political networks was as much a feature of the Message Movement as it was of al-Da'wa. The nephews of al-Shirazi were particularly active in the development of the political networks. In 1973, Hadi al-Mudarrisi, the younger brother of Mohammed Taqi al-Mudarrisi, settled in Bahrain after a fruitless venture in the Emirate of Sharjah, a constituent part of the UAE. He had good contacts with the al-Alawi family, rich merchants based in Manama, the capital of Bahrain, whom he had met in Karbala while they were performing a pilgrimage. The al-Alawi family was strongly committed to the organisation of popular religious rituals, and was also well connected to the ruling Al Khalifa dynasty in Bahrain, with the head of the family serving at the time as Minister of Finance. Thanks to their influence, Hadi al-Mudarrisi gained privileged access to the state-run media, and was even accorded Bahraini nationality. He was quickly able to gather around himself a small group of supporters, who set up an embryonic political party within the framework of a religious association, the Husseini Social Fund (*Al-Sunduq al-Husseini al-Ijtima'i*).[7]

In contrast to al-Da'wa, Hadi al-Mudarrisi took no part in the crisis that culminated in the dissolution of Bahrain's parliament in 1975, but the episode marked a clear turning point in his political thinking. While al-Da'wa continued to look for a political solution to the crisis, the Shirazists took a different view, that a solution could only emerge from a root and branch restructuring of the situation. Though they had as yet no strategy or definite goals, they began to issue militant tracts that were very hostile to the ruling dynasty. Some activists went to seek military training in southern Lebanon, either in PLO training camps or those of the Shia militia Amal, sending a clear signal that a coup d'Etat was not seen as out of the question.

In Saudi Arabia, an inhospitable land for Shias, the *marja'iyya* of Mohammed al-Shirazi and the Message Movement did not spread through the direct settlement of exiles. Instead, the recruitment of activists took place in Kuwait. It seems clear that the central figure in this process was Hassan al-Saffar (born 1958). Long recognised as the main opposition leader, he is today the leading figure of Shia political Islam in Saudi Arabia and the principal interlocutor of the regime over the liberalisation measures brought in with varying degrees of success since the 1990s. Hassan al-Saffar was a member of a merchant family from Qatif, the principal centre of Shia population in the Eastern Province of the country, where Saudi Arabia's oil reserves are also concentrated. In this region, before the discovery of oil in the 1930s, Shias were a majority. The growth of the oil industry, however, has brought a massive influx of population from other parts of the country, which has reduced the proportion of Shias in the Eastern Province to around a third at the present day. Different estimates of the whole Kingdom put the proportion of Shias at between 6 and 20 per cent, though in Saudi Arabia, as elsewhere in the Middle East, the category "Shia" is not recognised by the national census.

Hassan al-Saffar, who came from the heart of the Shia region of the Kingdom of Saudi Arabia, soon embarked on a clerical career, and began his training in Najaf in the early 1970s. Unlike others, he devoted himself to his studies and took little interest in politics. He did not move in al-Da'wa circles. He had met Mohammed al-Shirazi during a previous visit to Iraq, but al-Shirazi had already left the country and al-Saffar did not become politicised in Iraq. Nevertheless, like many other foreign students, whom the Iraqi Baath regime suspected on principle of working against its interests, al-Saffar was soon compelled to leave Najaf, moving on to Qom in Iran to continue his clerical training. In 1974, he joined Mohammed al-Shirazi's seminary in Kuwait and began to participate in political activity. He quickly became a key figure in the Shirazi organisation. Mohammed al-Shirazi sent him to Oman, where he laid the foundations of a political organisation that has now been dissolved. At the same time, he recruited activists during his regular trips to Saudi Arabia. Dozens of these were sent to Kuwait for both religious and political training, including Tawfiq al-Seif, Fawzi al-Seif (Tawfiq's brother), Hassan al-Khuweildi and Yusuf al-Mahdi, among others. Today, these are all senior figures within the principal Saudi Shia political faction. As in Bahrain, where the Shias also faced an authoritarian regime openly hostile to its Shia population, they did not shrink from the option of direct confrontation with the government, though unlike their Bahraini counterparts they never undertook military training.

During the 1970s, the Shirazists had therefore succeeded in expanding beyond the narrow confines of Karbala to form themselves into a transnational organisation. This has continued to grow, whether as a simple religious movement or as a political party, with bridgeheads today in North America, Europe, East Africa, Central Asia and Oceania. However, despite becoming a transnational network the Shirazists have maintained their original quarrel with the *marja'iyya* of Najaf. This conflict has been most serious in the Gulf, no doubt because the financial stakes involved are higher than elsewhere. In Kuwait and Bahrain, antipathy between al-Da'wa and the Shirazists has taken on its most vituperative form. There, the *marja'iyya* of Najaf, headed by Abu al-Qasim al-Khoei between 1970 and 1992, has gone to the extent of issuing tracts denouncing the *marja'iyya* of Mohammed al-Shirazi as illegitimate and drawing attention to what was described as the sinister nature of his activities. This is not merely incidental, as will be seen, as it throws light on the structure of the Shia political landscape in several Gulf countries.

Musa al-Sadr in Lebanon: A family story

The rise of Musa al-Sadr (1928–1978) at the head of the Shia community in Lebanon offers a further example of the role of transnational clerical networks in the emergence of Shia Islamic movements in the Arab countries. In particular, it demonstrates the importance of transnational family ties in the circulation of political ideas.

Musa al-Sadr was born in Qom. He was, however, a member of a prestigious clerical family, the Sharaf al-Din, from Jabal Amil in southern Lebanon. In the eighteenth century, at a time when the local Ottoman governor was persecuting Shias, part of the family settled in Najaf, while some went on to Iran to found a dynasty bearing the al-Sadr family name. Like so many other Iranian *ulama*, members of the al-Sadr family divided their time between Iran and Mesopotamia. In Najaf, thanks to their religious and political status, they became one of the most significant clerical families. Mentioning only the best known amongst them, they included Mohammed Baqir al-Sadr, who was the founder of al-Da'wa, and Mohammed Sadiq al-Sadr (1943–1999), who was a key religious and political figure in the 1990s. Mohammed Sadiq al-Sadr was the father of Muqtada al-Sadr (born 1973) the young cleric who has made himself a crucial figure in the political manoeuvres of the post-Saddam Hussein era in Iraq. Up to the present day, the various branches of the family have continued to establish ties of marriage with one another. Thus, Musa al-Sadr was simultaneously the cousin and the brother-in-law of Mohammed Baqir al-Sadr. He was also the cousin of Abd al-Hussein Sharaf al-Din (1873–1957), the leading religious dignitary in the southern Lebanese city of Tyre in the 1950s.

Though educated in the *hawza*, Musa al-Sadr was one of the first Shia religious students who also undertook university studies, taking a course in law and economics at the University of Teheran. In the latter half of the 1950s, he completed his religious education in the seminaries of Najaf, where he attained the highest level, permitting him to practice *ijtihad*, the independent interpretation of sacred texts. In Najaf, Musa al-Sadr was in contact with the reformist circles within which al-Da'wa was later created. He shared intellectual concerns as well as family ties with Mohammed Baqir al-Sadr, since both took a strong interest in economics, but also took the opportunity in Najaf to make contact with a number of Lebanese students, including Mohammed Shams al-Din, whose links with al-Da'wa have already been mentioned. After his return to Qom in 1958, Musa al-Sadr was among the most active of the young clerics. His family was already known for its activism against the Iranian Pahlavi dynasty, since his maternal grandfather Hussein Qumi (died 1945) had been one of the earliest to oppose reforms that threatened the status of the clergy. Amongst Musa al-Sadr's friends were some who later became central figures of the Islamic Revolution in Iran, such as Mohammed Beheshti (1928–1981), who rose to be head of the Supreme Court of the Islamic Republic and secretary-general of the Islamic Republican Party, established in 1979 to coordinate the Iranian revolutionaries.

Though Musa al-Sadr was therefore typical of the activist clerical circles in Iraq and Iran within which the earliest Shia Islamic movements originated, it was more his family links than his political connections that accounted for his extraordinary career in Lebanon. The al-Sadr of Iran had maintained their links with the Sharaf al-Din in Lebanon, and in particular with Abd al-Hussein Sharaf al-Din, the leader of the Shias of Tyre, in Jabal Amil, who had distinguished himself by his anti-French political militancy during the French Mandate over Syria and Lebanon that was in force from 1920 to 1943. During one of Abd al-Hussein Sharaf al-Din's visits to his extended family in Qom, he was struck by the ability and charisma of his cousin Musa al-Sadr, to the extent that he chose him as his designated successor as community leader in Tyre, which he became in 1959. In comparison with the experience of Ali al-Kurani, Mohammed al-Shirazi or Hadi al-Mudarrisi in the Gulf, however, Musa al-Sadr faced an additional drawback: in addition to his lack of knowledge of local conditions, he spoke Arabic only with a strong Persian accent, which he was never able to lose. In practice, however, his long-standing family ties with the Sharaf al-Din, together with his position in professional clerical circles, enabled him to overcome the handicap of his foreign origins. He was from the start seen by his Lebanese co-religionaries as a son of the soil who had returned to his own country after a long journey. He took Lebanese nationality in 1963.

Musa al-Sadr vanished in 1978 while travelling in Libya, where he was probably murdered by the Gaddafi regime. The mystery surrounding his disappearance certainly aroused millenarian sentiments amongst Shias, who did not fail to draw the parallel with the occultation from view of the "awaited" Imam.

However, the social and political initiatives with which Musa al-Sadr was identified were not halted by his disappearance at the height of his popularity, which served in fact only to reinforce them. Today, all Shia political figures in Lebanon lay claim to his legacy. His actions were crucial in a number of ways. First, he overthrew the established political order within the Lebanese Shia community with his denunciation of the power of the notables, mainly large-scale landowners, who held a monopoly over Shia representation in parliament. In addition, he restored the clergy, who had been undermined in Lebanon just as they had been in Iraq and Iran by the emergence of secular ideologies, to a key position in the political scene. With his establishment in 1973 of the Movement of the Deprived, which was transformed into the Amal militia with the outbreak of the Lebanese civil war in 1975, he helped to facilitate the entry into politics of figures from hitherto underprivileged social backgrounds. These included members of the new class of educated individuals who did not originate from the great notable families. One such, Nabih Berri (born 1938), who was a lawyer from the Lebanese diaspora in Africa, took the leadership of Amal in 1980 and was elected in 1992 as the Speaker of the Lebanese parliament, a position reserved for Shias within the Lebanese political system, which Nabih Berri continues to occupy to the present day.

Another achievement of Musa al-Sadr was to empower the Shia community in Lebanon to begin to transform its position within the Lebanese social and political system. Installed under the aegis of the French, the so-called Lebanese National Pact (*al-Mithaq al-Watani*) of 1943[8] was predicated on a strictly regulated division of power between the seventeen religious groups in Lebanon, dependent on a system of quotas governing representation in parliament and in the public service. Initially, this system was based on the demographic statistics of each community as reported in the census of 1932. At that time, the Maronites were most numerous, followed by the Sunni Muslims and then by the Shias. Within the framework of the Pact, the Maronites and the Sunnis, who included the merchant notables that dominated the country's economy, allocated themselves the two most powerful political institutions; the presidency of the republic and the position of prime minister, which have since been the preserve of the Maronites and the Sunnis respectively. The Shias, who were fewer in numbers and, more importantly, marginal in socio-economic terms, and without collective organisation, were allotted only the position of Speaker of Parliament, a position without real power.

Difficulties had already begun to emerge at the time when Musa al-Sadr began his effort to mobilise the Shias, since it had become common knowledge, even without a new census, that the demographic balance between the communities had begun to change, and that the Shias, if they were not already in a majority, were about to become so.[9] Despite this, in contrast to the attitude of Hezbollah, established in the early 1980s, which demanded a fundamental reorganisation of the political system, Musa al-Sadr and his movement did not seek, at least in the first instance, to upset the political and religious equilibrium. Their initial objective was to give the Shias the means of exercising greater influence in political negotiation. To that end, Musa al-Sadr set up the first institution to represent the Lebanese Shia community in 1967: the Higher Shia Islamic Council (*Al-Majlis Al-Islami Al-Shi'i Al-A'la*). This enabled the Shias to speak with a single voice when faced by the long-established Maronite and Sunni community organisations. The later establishment of the Movement of the Deprived was similarly motivated; its goal was not to challenge the system but to improve the position of the Shias within it.

3

THE ISLAMIC REPUBLIC OF IRAN

A DISPUTED MODEL

In February 1979, Ruhollah Khomeini returned to Iran after fifteen years in exile. He rapidly established himself as a charismatic figure in the revolutionary movement that had deposed the Shah, becoming the supreme political authority of the new regime in Teheran. This was an Islamic Republic, governed according to the doctrine of *wilayat al-faqih*, where the so-called "Guide of the Revolution" assumed all the key functions. It is not the intention of this book to rehearse once more such a well documented story. The objective here is rather to analyse the long term consequences of the establishment of the Islamic Republic for the Shia Islamic movements, both in Iran itself and in the countries that have been touched on in previous chapters. In fact, it was possible to speak of a phenomenon of "contagion" in the Middle East, spreading out from the revolutionary initiative of Iran, in which the Shia Islamic movements were the main protagonists. In practice, the Iranian leadership made it no secret: the export of the revolution was a central plank of their foreign policy, and impious regimes would be well advised to beware. What has become of this revolutionary dynamic today, and does the Iranian regime still provide a model for Shia Islamic activists? Furthermore, if the answer is in the affirmative, what is its significance?

The export of the revolution by the Shirazists

Ideologies and models of political action are seldom propagated by a simple process of indoctrination and imitation. The examples of al-Da'wa and the Shirazists have shown that it is travel by individuals and the personal connections which they create that facilitate the movement of ideas, and particularly the extent to which such ideas take root in any given society. In short, behind the spread of a political movement, to a country or a region, or in today's circumstances even throughout the world, lies a network of individual activists. Such networks are all the more effective where they make use of existing patterns of relationships that are historically well established. The Islamic Revolution is no exception. Its ideology was diffused through the long-established transnational clerical networks, and especially by way of the networks put in place by al-Da'wa and the Shirazists.

Mohammed Shirazi's networks were the first to put themselves at the service of the Islamic Revolution. There were a number of reasons for this. As has been pointed out, the leadership of al-Da'wa and the *marja'iyya* of Najaf in general were initially, due to their relationships with the regime of the Shah, in an ambiguous position as regards the Islamic regime. The Shirazists, on the other hand, did not experience this kind of diffidence, having long beforehand built a special relationship with Khomeini, and having also developed a theory of government by the clergy that was not far removed from his ideas. It is for this reason that, after 1979, many figures within the Shirazi movement settled in Iran, long before the officials from al-Da'wa to whom Iran later offered sanctuary following the assassination of Mohammed Baqir al-Sadr in April 1980. In the fervour that ensued after the revolution, when there was a proliferation of autonomous revolutionary groups over whom the Iranian government had little control, the Shirazists were especially active among the Arabic-speakers of Khuzistan. In this region, in which the chaos of the revolution opened the door to new separatist demands, the Shirazists, whose native Arabic enabled them to communicate easily with the population, took on the role of propagandists for the new ideology.

Though the Shirazists committed themselves to assisting the new regime in imposing its authority over its territory, they also had more ambitious plans. As they saw it, the Islamic Revolution in Iran was only a first step, and should be utilised as the jumping off point for the struggle against impious regimes that oppressed Shias, in Iraq in the first instance, as well as in Bahrain and Saudi Arabia. They agreed with those who took the view that the revolution would only be spread through force of arms, and hoped for logistical support from the new regime to embark on military operations. It should be stressed that this position was one which the Iranian revolutionaries were not unanimous on, many of them considering that the revolution could be spread simply through propaganda. In addition, the export of the revolution, in whatever fashion, was not a priority of the Iranian government, still at that time headed by moderates under the leadership of Mehdi Bazargan. Their main objective was to bring revolutionary activity under control in order to reaffirm the authority of the central government over proliferating factions and autonomous groups. On foreign policy, their priority was primarily to reassure neighbouring states that peaceful coexistence was an option. By the same token, they saw the revolutionary enthusiasm of the Shirazists as a danger.

It is this which explains why the Shirazists would continue to be closest to the most radical factions within Iran, and in particular that of Ayatollah Hussein Ali Montazeri (1922–2009), an associate of Khomeini who was to occupy the position of Khomeini's designated successor until 1989. Ayatollah Montazeri's son, Mohammed Montazeri, undertook military training in the Palestinian camps in Lebanon, specialising in armed operations. He established a personal relationship with Mohammed Taqi al-Mudarrisi, Mohammed al-Shirazi's nephew, who was the leader of the Message Movement. Al-Mudarrisi established links with Mehdi Hashemi (who died in 1987), the brother of Montazeri's son-in-law. After the death of Mohammed Montazeri in an armed attack in 1981, Mehdi Hashemi took charge of the Iranian Office for Liberation Movements, with the task of coordinating the activity of foreign revolutionary movements. The Office for Liberation Movements was a department of the Pasdaran, which was initially set up to safeguard the regime against its internal enemies but quickly became a key instrument for the export of the revolution. With the help of the Pasdaran, the Shirazists set up a radio station at Abadan, an Iranian city on the Gulf a few kilometres from the Iraqi frontier and close to the Arab monarchies. They initially broadcast programmes calling for the overthrow of Saddam Hussein and soon began to attack the Al Khalifa of Bahrain and the Al Saud of Saudi Arabia in similar terms.

The activities of the Shirazists would never have much impact inside Iraq, where they were swiftly overtaken, first by al-Da'wa and then by other groups that emerged in the 1980s. On the other hand, they were to have a crucial influence over events in Bahrain and Saudi Arabia. In the months that followed the Islamic Revolution in Iran, they announced the establishment of two movements whose names made clear their political programme. These were, first, the Islamic Front for the Liberation of Bahrain, officially led by Mohammed al-Alawi but within which Hadi al-Mudarrisi had the final say; and second, the Organisation for the Islamic Revolution in the Arabian Peninsula, led by Hassan al-Saffar. After an abortive attempt at popular mobilisation in Bahrain, Hadi al-Mudarrisi was deported and stripped of his Bahraini nationality. He then went to Iran, where he made plans for a coup d'Etat in Bahrain that would in the event result in the arrest and prosecution of the majority of the would-be plotters by the Bahraini authorities in 1981. In 1979, in Saudi Arabia, the Shirazists took the opportunity of the celebrations of the Shia festival of Ashura to mobilise the Shia population of the Qatif region, encouraging them to perform the Shia rituals associated with the festival in the open street. These had hitherto been tolerated by the Saudi government on the express condition that they should be confined to the interior of the *huseiniyyat* and the Shia mosques. In addition to the celebrants' unprecedented defiance of the prohibition, they also brandished pictures of Khomeini and chanted hostile slogans against the regime of the Al Saud. Dozens died in the subsequent action against the demonstration, sparking off a cycle of violence that lasted for several days, after which most of the leading figures in the Organisation for the Islamic Revolution in the Arabian Peninsula fled to Iran.

Iran's policy in Lebanon: The birth of Hezbollah

The activity of the Shirazists in Iraq and in the Gulf offers a striking example of how, in the chaotic circumstances of the revolution, and with the backing of the Iranian regime's most radical elements, an independently supported and financed Iraqi Shia Islamic movement was able to impose a foreign policy agenda on a reluctant central government in Iran. This is often alluded to by those hostile to the Shirazists, who frequently level the accusation that their aggressive anti-Iraqi propaganda provoked Saddam Hussein to attack Iran in 1980, and thus sparked off the Iran-Iraq war of 1980–1988. The Lebanese case relates to a different process, however, since in this instance what took place was not at the initiative of autonomous movements acting through radical factions in Iran, but was the result of the foreign policy of the central institutions of the Iranian government itself.

Iran did not, to be strictly accurate, export its revolution to Lebanon, but nevertheless, in Hezbollah, it provided itself with a particularly powerful means of exercising its influence. Because the Shirazi network had only a marginal presence in Lebanon, it played no part in the creation of Hezbollah. On the contrary, the role of the Lebanese activists of al-Da'wa was obvious, especially those who were members of a dissident group within Musa al-Sadr's Amal movement, known as Islamic Amal. The emergence of Hezbollah should be seen in the context of Amal's involvement in the Lebanese civil war which had been in full swing since 1975, and of the "disappearance" of Musa al-Sadr in 1978, some months before the Islamic Revolution. The resulting absence of leadership led to tensions and internal power struggles within Amal. Some were critical of the political and ideological direction of the movement, which, with the recent ascendancy of Hussein al-Husseini and Nabih Berri, had fallen under the control of lay officials. Such figures had always been in a majority in Amal's decision-making bodies, but had hitherto been eclipsed by the charismatic figure of Musa al-Sadr. Now, they took centre stage, giving the movement a new direction within which the objective of re-Islamisation was increasingly to be a side-issue. In the political sphere, Berri's goal was the "de-confessionalisation" of the Lebanese political system in favour of a classic political structure based on the principle of the democratic majority. In a context in which the Shias were now the largest community, "de-confessionalisation" was for Amal not only a sincere commitment to democratic universalism according to the principle of "one man, one vote", but also way to get a better deal for the Shias.

Meanwhile, under the auspices of Hussein al-Musawi, the dissidents of Islamic Amal also sought the de-confessionalisation of the political system, but challenged the secularisation of the party. Musawi and his colleagues were all clerics and were committed to the principle of clerical leadership of the party as well as to the goal of re-Islamisation. In contrast to Nabih Berri, they saw the Islamic republic of Iran as a model that could be transposed to Lebanon. In addition, Islamic Amal condemned the compromises made by the movement with the Israelis, who, after recurrent incursions into the Shia regions of southern Lebanon, had in 1982 installed themselves there permanently in order to establish a buffer zone between Israel and the Palestinian resistance. A priority for Islamic Amal was the continuation of the struggle against Israel with the ultimate objective of the total elimination of the Jewish state. The aim of Nabih Berri and his colleagues, on the other hand, was above all to eliminate any insecurity in the regions of Shia habitation in southern Lebanon that could be harmful to the civilian population. Clashes between the Israel forces and the Palestinian movements had already been severely detrimental in the south of the country. The economy of the region, basically agricultural, was threatened by the emphasis that the Lebanese merchant elite placed on the services sector, and had reached the last stages of decline, as thousands of Shias fled the insecurity of the region to find shelter in the suburbs of Beirut.

Hussein al-Musawi's position was in line with that of the historic leaders of al-Da'wa in Lebanon. For example, Mohammed Hussein Fadlallah soon took charge of those who saw the Islamic Revolution in Iran as a model. In 1982, together with others, including Subhi al-Tufayli, Raghib Harb and Mohammed Yazbek, Fadlallah attended the inaugural conference of liberation movements sponsored by Iran and held in Teheran. Such conferences were to be held regularly during the early years of the revolution with the aim of bringing together foreign revolutionary movements. In 1982, Khomenei exhorted the Lebanese to commit themselves without reservation to the struggle against Israel and the United States. Some months later, presumably on Khomeini's direct orders, Iran sent a contingent of Pasdaran to Lebanon, charged with setting up a new movement to be known as Hezbollah, literally, "The Party of God". The operations of the Pasdaran in Lebanon were run principally by the Iranian ambassador in Syria, Ali Akbar Mohtashemi, who later became Iran's Minister of the Interior.

The identities of those involved are an indication that the creation of Hezbollah followed a different model than that in operation in the activities of the Shirazists in the Gulf. First, Hezbollah was set up as the result of a policy formulated by the central government in Iran itself. The Iranian government always acknowledged its responsibility for its policy of intervention in Lebanon, while in the Gulf it never explicitly supported the Shirazists's activities. Hezbollah, for its part, made no secret of its expectation of financial and logistic support from Teheran. The specific nature of Iranian policy in Lebanon in contrast to that in the Gulf should be understood in the context of Lebanon's particular circumstances. Since Lebanon's inception as a country, it has lacked a central state authority able either to impose its authority on civil society or to prevent intrusion by foreign powers. One outcome of this was the presence within the territory of Lebanon of several different factions of the Palestine Liberation Organisation (PLO), whose numbers grew after their expulsion from Jordan in the early 1970s obliged them to make Lebanon their sanctuary and the base for their operations against Israel.

The outbreak of the Lebanese civil war in 1975 accentuated this tendency, as Lebanon transformed itself into a battlefield for regional powers, which confronted each other through Lebanese proxy militias. Israel and Syria were naturally involved, but also Iraq and Saudi Arabia which were Iran's two principal adversaries in the Arab world. Before the Islamic revolution, several movements opposed to the Shah of Iran had already established bases in Lebanon, including the Movement for the Liberation of Iran and also groups sympathetic to Ruhollah Khomeini that included his two sons, Ahmed and Mostafa. At the time, these formed part of a plethora of radical movements of many kinds who found their way to Lebanon to benefit from the expertise in guerrilla warfare of the armed Palestinian movements and the Lebanese militias. The creation of Hezbollah was therefore a matter of activating relatively long-established networks. In addition, Iran was not acting unusually in setting it up, since the Islamic Republic was doing no more than following the example of other neighbouring powers in providing itself with an instrument inside Lebanon whose influence would enable it to put pressure on its enemies. In addition to the states of the region, those western powers which had a significant military presence in Lebanon were also in Iran's sights: namely the United States and France. These two states, both of which supported the Iraqi war effort against Iran and had their own quarrels with Iran, became the object of attacks and hostage-takings that it was hoped would compel them to negotiate. The United States was later obliged to sell Iran arms that would prove decisive during the war with Iraq.[1] Meanwhile, France was in the end obliged to settle the issue referred to as the Eurodif affair.[2]

Iran never targeted the Lebanese state itself, weak and powerless as it was, and did not prioritise regime change in Lebanon or attempt to influence the country's internal politics. Though Hezbollah initially made the establishment of an Islamic republic in Lebanon one of its policy objectives, this was swiftly abandoned in the 1990s once the civil war was over. In contrast to Amal, which made efforts to play a part in Lebanese politics, Hezbollah, which saw itself above all as a jihadist movement opposed to Israel, simply ignored the Lebanese state. It was thanks to Hezbollah that Iran took on the role of a champion of the struggle against the "Zionist entity". Iran's policy in Lebanon, far from being regime change, was wholly at odds with the policy that the Shirazists would have liked to see Iran pursue in the Gulf, which was nothing less than the overthrow of the established regimes in Saudi Arabia and Bahrain. The effect of this policy was to give Iran the appearance of a power that sought to subvert the Arab countries, thus reinforcing the Arabs' view of it as an expansionist fundamentalist state. This was an image that Iran, on the other hand, would have preferred to shed, making alliances instead with such Arab states or political movements as were capable of assisting it against Iraq and the western powers. In this light, Iran's engagement in the struggle against Israel was instrumental in allowing it to strengthen its links with the Palestinian resistance on the one hand, and on the other hand to establish an alliance with Syria, with which Iran shared a strong hostility towards Iraq. These two axes continue to be basic facts of regional geopolitics up to the present day.

Hezbollah as a transnational network

Within Lebanon, Hezbollah created a bridge between the existing bedrock of al-Da'wa, headed by Mohammed Hussein Fadlallah, and a new generation of militants who had become politicised in the wake of the Islamic revolution, following a pattern in evidence in other countries in the Middle East. The name "Hezbollah" did not designate solely the Lebanese political organisation but also referred, in Shia Islamic circles, to a transnational network including, according to the country concerned, various sympathetic organisations and individuals. Such organisations and persons were in general linked by loose interpersonal links. They knew each other, and often met, but did not form part of a single command structure. Their personal backgrounds and political agendas sometimes differed widely according to their countries. Essentially, what brought them together was their recognition of the Islamic Republic of Iran as a political model, and their acceptance of the religious authority of the Guide of the Revolution, Ruhollah Khomeini, who was succeeded in 1989 by Ali Khamenei. Inside Iran, the expression "Hezbollah" also referred to those, sometimes organised into small pressure groups, who had taken it upon themselves to defend Khomeini's heritage against those they deemed to be counter-revolutionaries, and they did not hesitate to threaten and sometimes assassinate them. However, since the expression "Hezbollah" carried with it unsettling and even pejorative connotations for those who did not adhere to its ideology, these Hezbollah activists often referred to themselves as the partisans of the "Line of the Imam". The Imam in question here was not the Mahdi, whose return would signify the "End of Days", but Ayatollah Khomeini himself. Khomeini was often known as the "Imam", both to acknowledge his exceptional role in the history of Shiism, which serves as a model to follow,[3] and to hint at a special proximity between Khomeini and the Mahdi, or even at an identity between the two.

In the wider Arab world beyond Lebanon, there is only one organisation at present that openly acknowledges the name of Hezbollah, namely "Hezbollah in the Hijaz" (*Hizbullah al-Hijaz*) in Saudi Arabia. In that country, only marginally infiltrated by al-Da'wa, the predominance of the Shirazists in the sphere of Shia political Islam had remained unchallenged. "Hezbollah in the Hijaz", however, was created inside Iran by young Saudi students at the seminaries of Qom who rejected the leadership of the Shirazists. In 1983, headed by Hashim al-Shukhus (born 1957), they set up the Assembly of Ulama of Hijaz (*Tajammu' 'Ulama' al-Hijaz*), which by 1987 became "Hezbollah in the Hijaz", the name under which they claimed responsibility for attacks in Saudi Arabia and elsewhere. Specifically, Hezbollah in the Hejaz is suspected of responsibility for the attack on the American military barracks at Khobar in Saudi Arabia in 1996. The name "Hezbollah in the Hijaz" itself gives the clue to the organisation's political line. Hijaz is the western province of the Kingdom of Saudi Arabia, the site of the two holy cities of Mecca and Medina, which are the cradles of Islam. This is a region in which, however, there are only a very few

Shias, with those who exist being for the most part inhabitants of Medina. However, the activists of Hezbollah in the Hijaz are not native to this region, but originate from the eastern province of Saudi Arabia. The reference to "Hijaz" should therefore not be interpreted as a claim for autonomy on the part of activists agitating in the name of some specific regional identity. In fact, it is more a way of drawing attention to the sacred character of the Arabian Peninsula, while also flagging up a rejection of the way in which the Al Saud dynasty has appropriated the major part of the Arabian Peninsula. In this way, Hezbollah in the Hijaz simply follows the line laid down by Khomeini himself in his many speeches denouncing the Al Saud.

In contrast to Lebanese Hezbollah, which has over the years succeeded in establishing itself as an authentic popularly based political party, and which has by the same token complicated its relationship with its Iranian mentor, Hezbollah in the Hijaz has only ever had a small following in Saudi Arabia. It remains in practice no more than a tiny clandestine group, slavishly adherent to Teheran's policies. Its activities have been restricted to a handful of armed operations, together with belligerent pronouncements denouncing the Saudi regime. It counts few supporters in comparison with the Shirazists, who have, in contrast, been able successfully to move on into a post-revolutionary phase and become the Saudi regime's chosen Shia interlocutors.

In Kuwait, there is officially no "Hezbollah", though Kuwaitis familiarly refer to the National Islamic Alliance by this name. This movement, launched in 1998, includes, as in Lebanon itself, both former al-Da'wa members and younger activists, who were mainly drawn into political activity in Iran during their studies at the *hawza* of Qom. Such figures include Adnan Abd al-Samad, a leading figure of the movement, and Abd al-Muhsin Jamal, both of whom had in the 1970s been members of al-Da'wa, known at the time as the Social Association for Culture (*Jama'iyya al-Thaqafa al-Ijtima'iyya*). The secretary-general however, is a figure from the younger generation, Hussein al-Ma'tuk (born 1969), who was trained as a cleric in Qom in the 1980s. The Islamic National Alliance professes its adherence to the ideology of the Islamic Republic, and therefore to the doctrine of *wilayat al-faqih* and to the religious leadership of Ali Khamenei. In contrast to "Hezbollah in the Hejaz", however, it was, under different names, the most important political force among the Shia population of Kuwait throughout the 1980s and the 1990s. Since 2000, it has grown constantly weaker because of the fragmentation of the Shia political scene, which saw the emergence of numerous new political groups, all of them backed by the regime, while the Islamic National Alliance always identified itself as an opposition group. A severe blow was dealt to the movement in 2008 after its leaders miscalculated the impact of a rally they organised in order to celebrate and mourn Imad Mughniyya (1962–2008). Mughniyya, who had been a senior member of Lebanese Hezbollah and had been responsible for many of the party's armed attacks around the world, was assassinated in Damascus in February 2008. He was deemed to be responsible for at least one attack in Kuwait, the hijacking of an aircraft in 1988, and is suspected by many of having been behind others in the 1980s. The eulogy was hence considered by many in Kuwait as celebrating an enemy of the state and several senior officials of the National Islamic Alliance were arrested and detained for a few days, including members of parliament such as Adnan Abd al-Samad and the movement's general secretary, Hussein al-Ma'tuk. They were all released in the end, but the episode seriously undermined their credibility among the Kuwaiti Shias, many of who considered that they had contributed to spreading an incorrect image of Shias as disloyal citizens.

Despite this, however, the Islamic National Alliance is by and large a legalist political movement. Though it defines itself in opposition to the ruling Al Sabah dynasty, its objective is simply to curtail the power of the Al Sabah, while extending the powers of parliament, and like all other political factions in Kuwait it makes clear its commitment to the royal family. In particular, its leaders were not prosecuted in relation to the series of armed attacks that were perpetrated on Kuwaiti soil in the 1980s during the Iran-Iraq war by groups backed by Iran, most probably by a joint Hezbollah and Iraqi al-Da'wa venture in which Mughniyya played a role. Both foreign and Kuwaiti targets were hit. These included the American and French embassies; as well as the airport, the electricity and water ministry, the industrial zone, and various cafés, but crucially also the ruler himself, who narrowly escaped a machine gun attack on his car in 1985. The motivation for these incidents was broadly similar to that which lay behind similar operations carried out in Lebanon. Iran wished to bring pressure to bear on the United States and France for reasons already alluded to, and also sought to intimidate Kuwait itself, which, together with Saudi Arabia, was the main provider of funds for Iraq's war effort against Iran.

In Bahrain, Hezbollah remains no more than an idea, even according to those whose support it would have enjoyed. In other words, there is no organised structure, merely a series of individuals claiming allegiance to the legacy of Khomeini. Here again, there are both al-Da'wa veterans and a much younger generation of clerics educated at Qom. It is significant that Isa Qasim, an al-Da'wa leader from the 1970s, is seen in Shia Islamic activist circles as the principal representative of the Hezbollah tendency in Bahrain. Popular iconography, ubiquitous in the streets, is unambiguous on the issue. Pictures of Isa Qasim are displayed side by side with those of Ali Khamenei, Hassan Nasrallah and other leading figures of the "Line of the Imam", even though he has no official affiliation to any political party and has refrained even from declaring any religious allegiance to Iran, much less making an ideological commitment. Here again, the customary prudence towards political parties shown by those clerics who occupies the most senior positions in the religious hierarchy is in evidence.

What is the position in Iraq, however? From the 1980s onwards, small groups whose nature it is difficult to discern, have regularly laid claim to the label of "Hezbollah", but none of the key actors in Shia political Islam have been involved. After the overthrow of Saddam Hussein, a group bearing the name Hezbollah made its appearance, led by a man named Abd al-Karim Mohammedawi, but little information is available about it. On the other hand, the Supreme Council for Islamic Revolution in Iraq (SCIRI, which changed its name to the Supreme Islamic Council in Iraq from 2007)[4] shows all the characteristics of being an Iraqi Hezbollah. Mohammed Baqir al-Hakim (1939–2003), the son of the *marja'* Muhsin al-Hakim, established SCIRI in 1982, at the initiative of Iran. In 2003, Mohammed Baqir al-Hakim was assassinated, after which his brother Abd al-Aziz al-Hakim (1950–2009) took over as leader. SCIRI was initially intended as an umbrella organisation drawing together the various Iraqi resistance groups, but under the auspices of Abd al-Aziz al-Hakim and his brothers, it became a fully fledged organisation in its own right, recognising the authority of Ali Khamenei and adopting the concept of *wilayat al-faqih* as its governing principle. Its current leader is Ammar al-Hakim (born 1971), the son of Abd al-Aziz al-Hakim, who succeeded his father on his death in 2009. Its internal structure is in several ways similar to that of Hezbollah in Lebanon, especially in the discipline of its militias, the Badr brigades, who were trained by the Pasdaran during the years of exile in Iran. In this respect, it presents a striking contrast, for example, with Muqatada al-Sadr's militia, the Mahdi Army. This latter group, initially uninfluenced by the organisational culture of the Pasdaran, looks less like a tightly run military body than a collection of armed groups, relatively autonomous of a central authority that seems to be fairly indecisive.

SHIISM AND POLITICS IN THE MIDDLE EAST

Iranian foreign policy and the Shia movements

The establishment of the Islamic Republic undoubtedly inaugurated a process of the absorption of the Shia movements by Iran. Thanks to the Revolution, Iran regained in every sense its status as the centre of the Shia world. Even if Ayatollah Khomeini did not exercise a monopoly over religious authority, he enjoyed immense popularity outside Iran. Meanwhile, the seminaries in Qom, now in receipt of state funding, underwent an unprecedented expansion, while Iran became the refuge of choice and the tutelary power for the many Shia Islamic activists who were oppressed in their own countries and forced into exile. On the other hand, the attractive force of Teheran also generated centrifugal tendencies in reaction against it, which have resulted in a situation where today the Iranian model is no longer the object of a consensus among the Shia Islamic movements but has become a debating point and even an issue over which movements disagree.

The primary factor accounting for this phenomenon is undoubtedly the attitude of the various Shia movements to the foreign policy of the Islamic Republic. Al-Da'wa in Iraq is a case in point. In the late 1980s, having already undergone a number of schisms, the party faced its most serious internal dissent so far. The question at issue was precisely the nature of its relationship with Iran, and a related topic, the hierarchy of clerics and laymen in its decision-making bodies. After an initial period of indecision over its attitude towards the regime that had resulted from the Islamic revolution, al-Da'wa gave undivided support to the Islamic Republic. This was rapidly reinforced after the onset of the Iran-Iraq war in 1980 and the vigour with which the Ba'th Party crushed the Shia opposition in Iraq. As others had done before them, the officials of al-Da'wa at that point decided that Khomeini's Iran was the best place of sanctuary from which to pursue their political activities, rapidly establishing themselves as the central figures of the Iraqi Shia Islamic opposition in exile in Iran. In 1982, therefore, when SCIRI was formed, initially as an umbrella for a number of Shia opposition movements, al-Daʻwa found itself with the largest number of representatives within it. The Shirazists, took only one seat, which was indicative both of their lack of numbers within the territory of Iraq and of the tensions with the regime that were at that time appearing (see below).

Significantly, however, the cooption of al-Daʻwa by Iran was the cue for dissent within the party, which was further exacerbated by developments in the war with Iraq in the spring of 1982 that placed the Iraqi opposition in a difficult position. Up to then, Iraq had been the aggressor and Iran had merely defended its territory, which had been invaded. In early 1982, however, the Iranian army drove out the Iraqi troops and instead of accepting the cease-fire that Saddam Hussein then proposed, it opted to pursue the conflict and invaded the territory of Iraq, with the goal of the destruction of the Baathist regime. The Iraqi army, however, made a stand, and the war became bogged down, with neither side able to score a decisive victory. In this context, the Iraqi opposition ran the risk of appearing to be the ally of an expansionist foreign power, the obstinacy of which was standing in the way of a halt to the conflict and the destruction. It was also the case that, on the ground, the Iraqi troops, themselves mostly Shias, showed no religious or political solidarity with their Iranian coreligionists.

In practice, in many respects, the war only served to strengthen the misgivings that many al-Daʻwa officials had felt from the outset. The lay officials in particular had always been reluctant to sign up to a total alliance with Iran. In their view, al-Daʻwa was an Iraqi national party in exile. While it enjoyed Iran's political and logistic support, it should nevertheless be able to set its own autonomous agenda. The clerical officials, however, saw the issue of relations with Iran in an entirely different light, maintaining their refusal to recognise the force of nationalist arguments and framing their policies in terms of traditional religious ideas. For them, Khomeini was a *marja'* who had succeeded in establishing the first and only Islamic state, by virtue of which he deserved obedience in all respects. Logically, this led in the direction of greater integration between the party and the Iranian regime. These differences of position intensified to the point of an actual schism in 1988, when the *ulama* and the *effendis* parted company. The separation corresponded as much to a conflict between two types of protagonists with opposing political viewpoints as to a conflict over relations with Iran. It was indicative that the clerics, including such men as Kadhem al-Ha'iri, Mohammed Mahdi al-Asefi, and Murtada al-Askari (who died in 2007), remained in Iran, where they initially set up an organisation they named "al-Da'wa Council of Fuqaha", though they soon ceased to have any organised existence. However, some of them became members of influential Iranian political institutions. Mahmud al-Hashemi, for example, became a member of Ali Khamenei's staff in 1989, when Khamenei succeeded to the position of Guide of the Revolution, and in 1999 was appointed head of the judicial system. Ali al-Tashkiri, another member of Ali Khamenei's staff, was elected to the Council of Experts in 1999, also becoming head of Iran's Islamic Culture and Communication Organisation. He currently occupies an important position managing relations with foreign Shia movements, particularly, but not entirely, in connection with Iraq. The lay officials, by contrast, set up a body called the "Cadres of al-Da'wa" (*Kawadir al-Da'wa*), and tended to distance themselves from Iran, in both geographical and political terms, with many of them choosing alternative places of exile. Nuri al-Maliki, who became prime minister of Iraq in April 2006, went to Syria. Others chose Britain, which became the refuge of Ibrahim al-Ja'fari, Maliki's predecessor as prime minister of Iraq, who served from April 2005, and Muwaffaq al-Ruba'i, who served as the Iraqi government's National Security Adviser from 2004 to 2006.

The case of the Shirazists sheds light on another aspect of the impact of Iranian foreign policy decisions on the so-called "liberation movements". The goal of exporting the revolution, and the hard line adopted by the military, were only one facet of Islamic Iran's foreign policy. From the earliest days of the revolution, in fact, the radicals and the pragmatists had clashed over the broad lines of foreign policy. The radicals, often known as the "Islamic Left", owing to their ideological affinities with third-world movements, especially their economic policies, which could be characterised as "socialistic", were the most active proponents of the export of the revolution by force of arms. The pragmatists, on the other hand, who were known as the "Conservative Right", wanted to see a rapid transition from the revolutionary to the post-revolutionary state. They placed emphasis on the consolidation of the control of the central government over internal politics, while their foreign policy objectives were very traditional. In contrast to the radicals, of whom many remained attached to the notion that the revolution should lead to the entire foundation of the international system being called into question, the pragmatists aimed to occupy a position of power within the system as it existed. They had no desire to change the rules of the international game, but only to rearrange the balance of power. They had no objection to the use of threats, but preferred the exercise of influence. The pragmatists drew their conclusions from the misplaced destabilisation operations undertaken by the radicals, which had left Iran isolated on the international stage. It was necessary at all costs, as they saw it, to put an end to such a situation in order to re-establish good relations with all of Iran's neighbours, including even Iraq, with which Iran inaugurated a process of reconciliation towards the close of the 1990s.

In 1986, the Iran-Contra affair was the occasion for a decisive settling of scores between the radicals and the pragmatists. Initially supposed to be secret, the American arms sales to Iran were disclosed to the media by Mehdi Hashemi, who had played a leading role in the coordination of logistic and financial support to the liberation movements, and was also a close associate of Ayatollah Montazeri, who was still seen at the time as Khomeini's heir. Through his revelation of the existence of the Iran-American arms deal, Hashemi hoped to undermine the pragmatists, and in particular Ali Akbar Hashemi-Rafsanjani, who had played a central part in setting up the deal. His gambit turned out badly, since Khomeini lent his support to the pragmatists, openly accusing Mehdi Hashemi of endangering the Islamic Republic and eventually having him executed. In many ways, the downfall of Ayatollah Montazeri from his position of heir apparent in March 1989 was the final phase in the ousting of the radicals. With his fall from grace, an era in the history of Islamic Iran came to a close. The pragmatists were able henceforth to ensure that their ideas prevailed, and priority was placed on the reintegration of Iran into the international community. The end of the war with Iraq in 1988 facilitated the transition, which was completed in 1991 with the Gulf War, in which Iran gave unqualified support to the western coalition that drove Iraq's forces out of Kuwait. While some degree of antagonism remained, there was a marked improvement of relations with the Gulf monarchies, including Saudi Arabia.

The ousting of the radicals and the reorientation of Iranian foreign policy had drastic consequences for the Shirazists, and especially for the two brothers Mohammed Taqi al-Mudarrisi and Hadi al-Mudarrisi, as well as the various political movements they led, both in Iraq and in the Gulf. These movements, which, except in Saudi Arabia, had seen their political influence substantially diminished in a variety of fields of action, had staked everything on the radical factions within the Iranian regime in order to achieve the realisation of their plans. Closely identified with Mehdi Hashemi, they were even said to have been involved in the exposure of the American arms sales to

Iran.⁵ The elimination of Mehdi Hashemi saw their status transformed instantly from that of an influential movement to that of a group of troublesome extremists. In addition, the Bahraini government asked the government of Iran, as an earnest of good faith in the process of rapprochement in which it wished to engage, to close down the offices of the Islamic Front for the Liberation of Bahrain in Teheran and to withdraw its support, which it did with no apparent misgiving. The movements in Saudi Arabia suffered the same fate. Meanwhile, most of the Iraqi activists left Iran for Syria, where at least the infrastructure set up by Hassan Shirazi at Sayyida Zaynab in the 1970s was available to use as new headquarters. Subsequently, the Mudarrisi brothers set themselves up there, soon to be followed by the Shia activists from Bahrain and from Saudi Arabia. For all of them, dreams of revolution had vanished and the objective was instead to survive the failure of their political strategy. They not only needed to continue to play a political role but also, and perhaps more importantly, to identify a practical means of surviving as an organisation.

The Shia movements and quarrels within the marja'iyya

The second factor explaining the centrifugal impetus that took shape in reaction to the process of centralisation around Iran was the emergence of clashes over the religious authority of Khomeini, and a fortiori over that of his successor Ali Khamenei. An initial episode of this kind was the conflict that broke out yet again around the highly controversial personality of Mohammed al-Shirazi. It has been mentioned that al-Shirazi was one of the first in Iraq to lend his support to Khomeini and had developed political ideas very similar to his. Barely a few months after the revolution he established his headquarters in Qom, where Khomeini, as a mark of his recognition and respect, paid him a welcome visit. After this, however, relations between the two men went rapidly downhill.

A decisive element in their falling out was a difference of view over the conduct of political affairs, both internal and external. Ayatollah al-Shirazi was critical of the relentless persecution of those who opposed the new regime and the campaign of terror waged against "counter-revolutionaries". He also condemned the limitations placed on freedom of expression and on multi-party politics. Worse still, in Khomeini's eyes, he let it be known that he regarded the doctrine of *wilayat al-faqih*, as it was being implemented by the Guide of the Revolution, as a form of dictatorship contrary to the spirit of Islam. As he saw it, the Islamic state should be run by the clergy, but in a collegiate style, and his desire was to replace the Guide of the Revolution with a council of the *maraji'*. This was the doctrine he called *shurat al-fuqaha*, literally "The Council of the Doctors of Law". In the external sphere, al-Shirazi at first fervently backed the war against Saddam Hussein, which he regarded as the only realistic route to the deposition of the dictator and the installation of an Islamic regime in Iraq. Later, however, he concluded that the military option was not only ineffectual but was also discrediting the Iraqi opposition in the eyes of its supporters in Iraq. This would later become the basis for his views on non-violence, which was later to be a central element in his political thought.

The significance of the clash between Ayatollah Khomeini and Ayatollah al-Shirazi is not of merely anecdotal interest. It also reveals a structural tension between the mode of functioning of the *marja'iyya*, as constituted in Mesopotamia in the nineteenth century, and the monopolistic nature of the *wilayat al-faqih*. On the one hand, the *marja'iyya* was a pluralistic institution, characterised by ongoing rivalries between those who laid claim to supreme religious authority, whether expressed in courteous or more antagonistic terms. On the other hand, the Guide of the Revolution not only had the final word in political decision-making, but also claimed a monopoly over religious authority. However, Mohammed al-Shirazi, in common with others, regarded Ruhollah Khomeini as an equal and not as his superior in the hierarchy. As he saw it, the fact that Khomeini had become Iran's Head of State had no impact on his position within the religious institution.

Supported by the power of the state, Khomeini had at his disposal a level of coercive force with which to impose his authority, that was unprecedented in the history of the *marja'iyya*. Mohammed al-Shirazi was nevertheless, despite his critical stance, able to pursue his activities during Khomeini's lifetime in a relatively unrestricted fashion. This was, it must be admitted, due to the fact that his audience in Iran was very limited, restricted as it was to refugees from Iraq of Iranian origin and more specifically to those expelled from Karbala. His pronouncements had little impact on internal politics, even more so since al-Shirazi had decided not to make his criticisms public in any systematic way, reserving them instead for his entourage and those who came to his seminaries. Other high-ranking clerics, on the other hand, whose religious and political standing in Iran was much greater, were obliged to pay the price for their dissent. The best known such instance is that of Mohammed Kazem Shariat-Madari (1905–1986). He had known Khomeini from student days in the seminary and had backed him in the 1960s when he first began to speak out against the Shah, subsequently playing an important part in the revolution through his support for anti-Shah demonstrations. In contrast to Khomeini, however, he took the view that a constitutional monarchy under which the clergy would exercise a simple power of veto would be satisfactory as a political system. From the earliest days of the revolution, he showed himself to be critical of the policies of the new regime. Denouncing the demands of the revolutionaries, and the excessive ideological proximity of some of them to the ideas of the left, he gathered around him what began to amount to a movement of malcontents, especially in his home region of Azerbaijan. In 1982, together with Sadeq Ghotbzadeh, he was accused of complicity in an attempted coup d'Etat, after which he was placed under house arrest by Khomeini and finally stripped of his status as a *marja'*. This was unprecedented in the history of the *marja'iyya*, where the status of *marja'* is not bestowed by any formal procedure, and Shariat-Madari's demotion provides a clear example of the way that the Islamic regime tried to absorb the religious institution.

Until Khomeini's death, this process of absorption appeared to function more or less as he intended, with his rivals, whether declared or potential, reduced to silence. In 1989, however, Khomeini's death soon exposed the limitations of the state's bid to exercise a monopoly in the field of religion. Having stripped Mohammed Hussein Montazeri of his status as heir to the position of Guide to the Revolution, Khomeini found himself in a dilemma as to who would be his successor. With Montazeri now in the opposition camp, and given the hostility of the Grand Ayatollahs of Qom to the doctrine of *wilayat al-faqih*, even though they did not express it in public, there was no longer a *marja'* capable of succeeding him. The institution of Guide to the Revolution, which was based on an amalgamation of temporal power and spiritual authority, was therefore at risk; and with it the entire religious authority of the Iranian regime. Khomeini's response was to ask for the constitution to be revised to allow the separation of the function of *marja'* from that of Guide. In the new constitution of 1989, the status of *mujtahid*[6] continued to be essential to fulfil the position of Guide. However, it was no longer necessary for the Guide to be a *marja'*, that is, to be recognised by one's peers as a scholar of sufficient wisdom to be deemed worthy of emulation by both lay people and clerics of inferior rank. The principal quality of the Guide, rather than his religious knowledge or his position in the religious institution, should henceforth be his political skill. In this context, some months before his death, Khomeini designated Ali Khamenei as his successor. Khamenei, who had since 1981 been President of the Republic, had wide political experience but, as was generally agreed, his religious knowledge was relatively limited and insufficient even to enable him to practise *ijtihad*. It is said by some that Khomeini, on his deathbed, resolved the problem by conferring upon Khamenei the status of *mujtahid*.

It is significant that it was under Khamenei's administration, when the religious legitimacy of the regime was at its weakest, that repression of the religious institution was intensified. In 1995, Khamenei, who had at first been content to present himself as a *mujtahid* but still did not claim the status of *marja'*, at last presented himself as a candidate for the supreme *marja'iyya* in Iran. His name appeared on a list published by the Association of Teachers at the *hawza* of Qom. This was an institution set up by the teachers at Qom in the 1960s, which, among other things, was intended to formalise the procedure for access to the *marja'iyya* through the validation of candidatures of religious scholars. After the revolution, it fell under the authority of the Guide and contributed to the legitimisation of the idea of a single supreme *marja'iyya* which would be exercised in Iran. In reaction to the outcry that greeted the publication of his name in the list of *ulama* capable of being designated as the supreme *marja'*, Khamenei responded that in the last resort pluralism was acceptable in the field of religious authority and that there was in fact no need for a unique *marja'*. In other words, he regarded himself as a *marja'* but did not intend to claim authority over his peers in Iran. On the other hand, he later claimed the status of *wali amr al-muslimin*, the "head of the Muslims", which in practise meant that he wished to assert supreme religious and political authority over Shias outside Iran. While this placated most of the Ayatollahs of Qom, it aroused furious reactions from those who, from their bases in Qom, Najaf or Beirut, were the leaders of networks of institutions and communities of the faithful throughout the Shia world.

It was logical that Khamenei's various strategies for the imposition of his religious authority should be accompanied by a campaign of intimidation against the most recalcitrant and the most vulnerable. Pressure against Ayatollah Montazeri, who had reacted to Khamenei's pretensions by calling for the Guide to be elected directly by the people, was stepped up. However, since Montazeri had retained significant influence within certain institutions, especially the Pasdaran, and as his following among the Iranian people was not inconsiderable, the campaign was directed instead against figures that were of lesser importance in Iran but led sizeable networks abroad. Mohammed al-Shirazi was a perfect case. Without a popular base in Iran, he was viewed with hostility by the establishment in Najaf, which was certainly unwilling to mobilise in his defence, and had based his entire strategy of achieving religious authority on the construction of transnational networks with their heart in the rich monarchies of the Gulf. He was the object of continuous harassment on the part of the Guide's henchmen, who compelled him to halt virtually all his teaching. His supporters were driven out and several of his sons were arrested and tortured. In December 2001, when he died, the regime's thugs seized his body in order to prevent his interment at his house in Qom, thus forestalling the eventuality that his tomb could become a place of assembly for his followers, who worshipped his memory. They buried him instead in a corner of the mosque which contained the sanctuary of Fatima, as was the tradition for high-ranking *ulama* in Qom. This gesture, though ostensibly it recognised his status as a Grand Ayatollah, was actually intended to obstruct Mohammed al-Shirazi's ultimate strategy to gain distinction by reducing him to the same level as the hundreds of other Grand Ayatollahs who were already buried at the mosque. In addition, in 2005, access to the area where he was interred was restricted to women, reducing yet further the possibility that any gathering might be held.

The struggle for control over the *marja'iyya* embarked upon by Khamenei represented the final phase of the rupture of relations between the Shirazists and the Islamic Republic. Its consequences were felt particularly by the Shia Islamic movements in the Gulf states, whence the Shirazists drew their main financial support and where they had remained highly active in both the political and religious fields. In these countries, the conflict that had originally opposed the Shirazists and al-Da'wa in the 1970s had taken a new direction. Amongst the former al-Da'wa activists, who had, as has been noted, mainly joined the pro-Iranian Hezbollah camp, the criticism that was directed at the Shirazists mainly concerned the issue of treason to Iran. Through their consistent challenges to the authority of the Guide, Ali Khamenei, the critics alleged, the Shirazists were undermining the world's only Shia state, and by the same token were acting to the detriment of all Shias. The response of the Shirazists was to condemn the subservience of their adversaries to the interests of Iran, which treated them virtually as a "fifth column". In Kuwait, the Shirazists had attempted since the late 1990s to organise a common front of anti-Iranian Shia political forces. In fact, in 2006, a wide front of Shia political and religious movements was set up in Kuwait, largely at the instigation of the Shirazists, which included all groups excepting Hezbollah (i.e. the National Islamic Alliance).

In 1995, another development took place that illustrated the readjustments within the Shia Islamic movements outside Iran that followed Khamenei's assumption of power. This was the proclamation of the *marja'iyya* of Mohammed Hussein Fadlallah. Because this was tantamount to a refusal to recognise Khamenei's claim to religious leadership outside Iran, Fadlallah's accession to the status of *marja'* was seen as a challenge on his part. This rebellious gesture went down badly with Iran because of the questions it raised over Iran's interests in Lebanon, where the Islamic Republic had at last won the majority of his supporters and, through Hezbollah, gained a lasting influence. In addition, Fadlallah's close links with Hezbollah meant that internal clashes could lead to a split within Hezbollah between pro-Khamenei and pro-Fadlallah factions. The stakes were raised yet higher when Fadlallah, not content with merely proclaiming his *marja'iyya*, also expressed his misgivings in relation to the doctrine of *wilayat al-faqih*, thus calling into question the political regime in Iran itself. In the end, Hezbollah did not split, as its activists, well aware of implications of a split with Iran that would be detrimental to Hezbollah's interests, remained faithful to the *marja'iyya* of Ali Khamenei. However, there was a fissure between Hezbollah and Fadlallah, even though many members certainly accepted his *marja'iyya* on an individual basis. Collectively, however, Hezbollah in Lebanon followed the *marja'iyya* of Khamenei.

Some of the lay officials of al-Da'wa, who had already distanced themselves some years before from Teheran, seized on the occasion of the proclamation of the *marja'iyya* of Fadlallah as an opportunity to attempt to reassert the erstwhile religious legitimacy of the "Cadres of al-Da'wa", the lay faction of the party. Though al-Da'wa did not officially recognise any particular *marja'*, permitting its activists a free choice in the matter, some were certainly irritated by the criticisms of those who accused them of being a party without a *marja'*, whose policies therefore ran the risk of deviation from the religious law. This group let it be known that they would place their faith in the views of Mohammed Hussein Fadlallah. This is the sense in which, in Shia Islamic circles, it is sometimes said that Mohammed Hussein Fadlallah was the "*marja'* of al-Da'wa".

The succession crisis in Iran had important consequences, therefore, for the Shia movements abroad. Indeed, Ali Khamenei had failed to impose his *marja'iyya* both internally and externally. On the contrary, his bid for the leadership of the broader Shia world actually created a deep split between pro and anti-Iranian factions. This split actually dates from the earliest days after the revolution, since the most eminent members of the Shia clergy, both in Iran and abroad, failed to adhere to the *wilayat al-faqih*, and with their rejection of the doctrine also refused to recognise the religious and political pre-eminence of Khomeini. However, with the struggles for the *marja'iyya* that took place after the accession of Khamenei to the position of Guide, a new factor nevertheless emerged. The Shia Islamic movements, whose enthusiasm had been aroused by the revolution, were in due course polarised into those who accepted and those who rejected the Iranian model.

Iran: The pros and the antis

Today, therefore, Shia political Islam is characterised by a profound polarisation between pro-Iranian and anti-Iranian factions. But to what precisely do these categories correspond? Any response to this question demands an analysis of the role of religious authority in the political decision-making process within each separate movement. On the matter, the practice does not necessarily follow avowed ideology. Before approaching this difficult issue, and in conclusion to this chapter on the Iranian model, analysis will be restricted to two issues. The first of these is that those movements which proclaim their hostility to the Iranian model do not in reality subscribe to a conception of the relation between politics and religion that differs in substance from that accepted by those who support the doctrine of *wilayat al-faqih*. The disciples of Mohammed al-Shirazi, for example, are ready to put forward his doctrine of *shurat al-fuqaha* as a democratic alternative to *wilayat al-faqih*. On the other hand, their wish to see the state run by a council of *maraji'* rather than by a single *marja'* does not constitute a challenge to the principle that ultimate power rests with the clergy. In reality, the conflict between the Shirazists and the Islamic Republic is not ideological. From one point of view, it relates to a classic pattern of competition for the *marja'iyya*, such as has existed since the institution came into being. From another standpoint, it is the result of rivalry between various centres of power in Iran and the political failure of those who supported the export of the revolution by force of arms. Thus, if some Shirazists condemn the Iranian regime as a dictatorship with nothing Islamic about it except the name, others carry on with the attempt to coexist with whatever faction has, for now, the upper hand within it. The brothers Mohammed Taqi al-Mudarrisi and Hadi al-Mudarrisi, having prudently distanced themselves by taking up residence in Syria, in the end reached a modus vivendi with some of the leading figures of the regime, who had previously eliminated some of their colleagues. After the fall of Saddam Hussein in 2003, Mohammed Taqi al-Mudarrisi went back to Karbala, but his brother Hadi continued to spend his time mainly in Teheran. In 2005, before the presidential elections that brought Mahmud Ahmadinejad to power, he made no secret of his hope for the return to power of Ali Akbar Hashemi-Rafsanjani, the right-wing leader who, in the 1980s and 1990s, had been behind the pragmatic foreign policy that had put an end to his hopes of revolution in Bahrain. Meanwhile, from Bahrain, Hadi al-Mudarrisi's erstwhile colleagues in the Islamic Front for the Liberation of Bahrain, now dissolved, levelled criticisms at the Iranian regime, not so much because it was undemocratic as because it had abandoned its original allies, the "real revolutionaries", in favour of a new wave of opportunists. In short, their attitude was more that of a betrayed lover than of a political adversary, and an antagonism that was apparently ideological concealed the failure of a political strategy.

The second observation is that those movements that declare themselves explicitly to be pro-Iranian, or are regarded as such, tend in fact to show a fierce independence with respect to Teheran. In other words, a "pro-Iranian" movement may follow a wholly autonomous agenda as concerns internal political affairs within the country in which it operates. The case of Bahrain is a paradigm. In Bahrain, al-Da'wa ceased to exist on an organised basis in 1984, following an agreement reached with the government, which, after the failed coup d'Etat by the Shirazists in 1981, had launched a massive wave of arrests in which al-Da'wa was not spared. Even though al-Da'wa activists had not been involved in the plot, the evidence they had given of support for the Islamic Republic had been enough to unsettle the Bahraini government. However, in contrast to the Bahraini Shirazists, most of the al-Da'wa activists decided either to stay in Bahrain, forswearing political activity, or to take up residence in Britain. Here again, the divergence between the courses of action of the clergy and the laymen was marked. While the clerics stayed in Bahrain, the laymen chose exile, though not in Iran. Like their Iraqi counterparts, they supported the Islamic Republic and mostly recognised the *marja'iyya* of Khomeini. However, they made a point of keeping their distance so that their political activity would not be discredited in the eyes of their compatriots, who did not want to see their country drawn into the orbit of Iran any more than did the Iraqis.[7] They were jealous of their independence, with democracy as their central political demand rather than the establishment of an Islamic regime modelled on that of Teheran. In 1982, they set up a new organisation that is still active in Bahrain today, the "Islamic Bahrain Freedom Movement" (*Harakat Ahrar al-Bahrain al-Islamiyya*—literally "Islamic Movement of Liberals in Bahrain").

4

THE POST SADDAM ERA

The immediate consequence of the diminished influence of the political model of the Islamic Republic within the Shia Islamic movement as a whole is that the foreign policy of Iran, in contrast to the situation that prevailed in the 1980s, is now only seen as a secondary factor in the analysis of Shia parties and groups. Iran's recently more pragmatic foreign policy has opened the way for Iran's political influence to be decoupled from the export of its political system. For the same reason, the Shia movement has begun to be seen as less of a threat by regional states. The events of 11 September 2001 and the emergence of Al-Qa'ida have reinforced this tendency, since the gravest terrorist danger now seemed to come from within the core of Sunni orthodoxy. The revolutionary potential of Shia political Islam seemed to be exhausted.[1] Moreover, the process of political liberalisation embarked upon in the Arab world in the 1990s, intermittently encouraged by the policies of President George W. Bush, president of the United States from 2000 to 2008, provided new opportunities for the Shia movements to influence the course of events through participation in existing institutions in their respective countries. At the same time, the policies of the Shia movements themselves began to consist essentially of reactions to the individual socio-political systems within which they had developed. In other words, in contrast to the 1970s and 1980s, during which considerations relevant to the region as a whole predominated, the period from 1990 to 2005 was characterised by a clear reorientation towards what could be described as the "domestification" of the political concerns of the Shias.

Why pick 2005 as the close of a period? Certainly, 2005 was a turning point in the way Shia issues were reported in the international press. The trigger was undoubtedly provided by the elections in Iraq in January and December, which democratically endorsed the Shias' accession to power in Iraq, putting an end to the tenuous hope that it might prove possible to organise the political system in that country in some way other than around communal divisions. In addition, during 2005, the violence in Iraq changed in nature. Initially directed against the coalition forces, it gradually evolved into a clash between militias recruited from the various communities, and in particular between Sunnis and Shias. Predictably, Iraq's democratisation took on the form of a settling of accounts between Sunnis and Shias, with the Sunnis making a bid to gain by violent means the political influence they had failed to win at the ballot box. It was also at this time that observers drew attention to the growing Iranian ascendancy in the Shia regions of Iraq, especially in the southern areas around Basra where the frontier with Iran seemed so permeable as sometimes scarcely to exist. In addition, the year 2005 also represented a turning point in Lebanon, with the murder in February of Rafiq al-Hariri and the reinforcement of the axis linking Hezbollah to Syria and Iran. Finally, in June 2005, the election of Mahmud Ahmadinejad as president of the Islamic Republic of Iran inaugurated a new phase in the perception of Shiism. This came at a moment when the international community had hoped for, and predicted, a win for Ali Akbar Hashemi-Rafsanjani that could have seen the inauguration of a much-desired process of reconciliation between Iran and the United States.

THE POST SADDAM ERA

The year 2005 was therefore marked by a conjuncture of events that, when taken together, gave the impression of a more or less coherent shift, which, some analysts suggested, was steered by Iran. Overall, the "regional" aspect of the Shia problem seemed once more to have taken the upper hand over the "domestic". The question must be, however, how real was this phenomenon, and had the policies of the Shia movements begun once more primarily to reflect regional considerations?

The Iraqi Shia movements and Iran from 2003: From ideology to tactics

Post-Saddam Hussein Iraq is the case most widely understood in terms of regional issues. Two scenarios predominate. The first is based on the presumption that developments in Iraq will affect neighbouring countries. On this analysis, were democratisation eventually to succeed, it would be an impetus towards democratisation for neighbouring regimes, and could become a powerful model for the Shia movements in other countries. Were it to fail, however, with the country lurching into civil war, Iraq would still serve as an example, if only one to be avoided. In addition, Iraq's intercommunal conflicts could still overspill its frontiers. The alternative analysis, seen as existing in parallel to the first rather than as an alternative to it, lays stress on the similarity of the situation of Iraq to that of Lebanon, as a focal point where regional dynamics could meet and interact. These included transnational Sunni jihadism, the so-called "American moment" in the Middle East,[2] the Kurdish question, the Sunni-Shia conflict, and, of course, Iran's bid for hegemony.

It is at this final point that we shall look first, followed by the consequences were events in Iraq to spill over elsewhere. Iran's foothold in Iraq is an established fact confirmed by the evidence of press reports, scholarly research and conversations with actors on the ground. Pictures of Khomeini and Khamenei are ubiquitous, with a multiplicity of religious organisations, and cultural or charitable associations that probably serve as a cover for Iran's various security and information services. Why Iran's ascendancy has occurred demands an explanation, and the question must be asked, is it a simple consequence of the religious and ideological affinities between Iraq's new masters and the Islamic Republic?

It has been pointed out in the previous chapter that certain Iraqi Shia organisations, especially al-Da'wa, have for some time distanced themselves in ideological and political terms from Teheran. There are at present indications that this tendency is gaining ground and is spreading to other movements. In other words, Iran has established its foothold in Iraq in spite of, and not because of, the Iraqi Shia organisations. Ibrahim al-Ja'fari and Nuri al-Maliki, the two prime ministers of the post-Saddam Hussein era, both emerged from al-Da'wa organisation known as "The Cadres of al-Da'wa" which included most of the lay officials of the party and had its origins in a clash with the clerical branch. Apart from the refusal of the *effendis* to accept the clerics' claim to supreme authority within the party by simple virtue of their status, they also rejected, in a related issue, the submission of the party to the authority of the office of the Guide of the Revolution that the clerics would have wished to see. To sum up, the remnants of al-Da'wa, which effectively headed the government of Iraq from 2005, were not pro-Iranian but adhered to policies that were national and Iraqi.

The transformation undertaken by the Supreme Council for Islamic Revolution in Iraq in 2007 shows that the path chosen by al-Da'wa some considerable time ago has been influential even within this most pro-Iranian of the Iraqi political organisations. The nature of this development within SCIRI, an organisation that came into being during the years of its leaders' exile under the shadow of Iran, was the result of its lack of a social base that could stand comparison to that of al-Da'wa. Though the suppression of al-Da'wa in Baathist Iraq and its years in exile have curtailed its support to the extent that even today it still cannot be considered a mass movement, it nevertheless has a history in Iraq and enjoys a resulting legitimacy, both of which SCIRI lacks. In other words, SCIRI could not have kept its position in the field of Iraqi politics without Iran's patronage and for it to keep its distance from Iran would have been pointless. In the immediate aftermath of the fall of Saddam Hussein, Iran's support was crucial in compensating for SCIRI's lack of a social base. In this respect, its most effective instrument was undoubtedly the notorious Badr Brigade, the SCIRI militia formed and trained by the Pasdaran, which was said at the time of the fall of the Baathist regime to have a membership of around 10,000 men. In the context of the unstable security situation created by the inability of the coalition forces to re-establish a central state with sovereign powers, especially including control over the exercise of violence, SCIRI undoubtedly found that such a force was a valuable asset in making its presence felt in the field of politics. The Badr Brigade, however, could not continue without Iranian military support.

In May 2007, what SCIRI embarked upon, notwithstanding its heavy dependence on Iran, was a spectacular ideological reorientation. This took the form of a proclamation at the party's annual general meeting of a change of name to the Supreme Islamic Iraqi Council (SIIC). In short, it abandoned all reference to the export of the Islamic Revolution and therefore any ambition to transfer the Iranian political model to Iraq. In practice, such a reorientation had already been signalled by SCIRI's actions. In media interviews, its leaders had already on a number of occasions pointed out that the specific nature of the Iraqi social situation, characterised by religious diversity, ruled out the establishment of an Islamic Republic in Iraq. SCIRI had already agreed with al-Da'wa, with the backing of Ayatollah Ali al-Sistani, that though clerics could be appointed as ministers, the prime minister should be a lay person. This policy was calculated to reassure the international community, which was uneasy over the links between the Iraq Shia Islamic movements and Iran, and the kind of Iraqi regime that could result. In the view of al-Da'wa and that of the United Iraqi Alliance, the front grouping together various Shia organisations which won the elections of 2005, Iraqi government policy should certainly accord with Islamic law, but it should in no way be subject to the approval of the clergy through the mechanism of any institutional machinery. For Ali al-Sistani, who was directly involved with the forging of the United Iraqi Alliance and had agreed to be its figurehead, this decision reflected his strongly felt view that the role of the clergy was not to run a government, as this could end only in undermining the credibility of the religious institution. As has been seen, this is the historic and majority position of the Shia clergy.

At the same time as the change of SCIRI's title to SIIC was announced, the party also made it known that it was placing itself under Ali al-Sistani's religious authority. This was entirely consistent with the change of name: with the abandonment of its endorsement of the Iranian political model, SIIC also renounced its support for the *marja'iyya* of Ayatollah Khomeini's successor, Ali Khamenei, who, as the custodian of the doctrine of *wilayat al-faqih*, was the embodiment of the specific nature of Iran's political system. In the context of the vigorous debate over Khamenei's *marja'iyya* after he succeeded Khomeini, and of his intense efforts to reaffirm his legitimacy outside Iran, this decision can only have been made after weighty deliberation. The SIIC was not, of course, asserting that Ali Khamenei is not a *marja'*, but nevertheless the expression of a preference for Ali al-Sistani amounted to an affirmation that al-Sistani is a greater scholar than Khamenei. Though most Shias would not see this as controversial, this declaration was a real snub for the Guide of the Revolution. This was even more the case in the circum-

THE POST SADDAM ERA

stances following the fall of Saddam Hussein, which Ali Khamenei clearly thought would be favourable to his interests, enabling him to have direct access to the *hawza* of Najaf and to subvert al-Sistani's influence there. After the fall of the Baathist regime, Khamenei embarked on a real offensive in Iraq to win a share of support from his rival, for example offering higher emoluments than al-Sistani to Najaf's seminary students. It is among the duties of the various *maraji'* to provide a stipend to students, who are entitled to seek donations from all the *maraji'*, whichever seminary they are attached to. Because al-Sistani is the most followed *marja'* in the Shia world and therefore receives the largest portion of the religious taxes paid, he had hitherto made the largest payments in Najaf, though closely followed by Khamenei. With the resources of a state behind him, however, Khamenei had no difficulty in reversing this in the course of 2006. It appears that this rivalry did not escalate, though with the two men reaching a kind of gentlemen's agreement where both respected each other's territory. In Najaf, al-Sistani provides stipends similar to those of Khamenei, while in Qom Khamenei provides the highest ones.[3]

Insufficient information has so far emerged on which to base a more detailed analysis of the causes and consequences of the change of SIIC's direction. A hypothesis may be formulated, however: it seems the change could not have been carried out without the agreement of the Iranian regime, and by the same token, it cannot be interpreted as a total breach with Iran. As has been pointed out, Iranian military support is essential to the Badr Brigade and the political cost of a break in relations would be too great. It remains to be revealed, however, with which of the rival centres of power that make up the Iranian regime there may have been consultation. Clearly, the change in *marja'iyya* could not have been approved by Ali Khamenei himself, or only with reluctance. The implication of this is that negotiation must have taken place with non-clerical factions within the regime, such as the presidency or the services that answer to it, specifically the intelligence services and the foreign ministry, but also no doubt some segment of the Pasdaran, from which Mahmud Ahmadinejad himself has emerged. Such actors were relatively unengaged with the contest for the *marja'iyya* and took a relatively pragmatic approach to external policy, in which the identity of the *marja'* and the *marja'iyya* were of limited importance provided that there was a consensus of interests and that Iran could bring to bear sufficient pressure to impose its will. According to this logic, it would actually be preferable for the *marja'* to be someone who refuses to align himself automatically with Iran in order to preserve his legitimacy in Iraqi eyes, as such a person, who remained independent from Iran, could be a useful arbiter at key moments. In other words, the process of "Iraqisation" of the former SCIRI was good for Iran, to the extent that it was intended to reinforce SCIRI's influence on the Iraqi scene. All this accords perfectly with the pragmatic change of direction of Iranian foreign policy that took place in the late 1980s, where alliances were henceforth to be built on tactical rather than ideological foundations.

The phenomenon of the "Sadrists" provides confirmation of the theory that the Shia Iraqi movements are in fact becoming increasingly domestic in their thinking and that their relations with Iran are becoming essentially tactical in nature. The emergence of the Sadrists was symptomatic of the realignments of the Shia political scene inside Iraq in the closing years of the Baathist regime. Muqtada al-Sadr, who gave his name to this heterogeneous movement, used his family connections to set up what has become "Iraq's first political party".[4] He is the only surviving son of Mohammed Sadiq al-Sadr (1943–1999), a distant cousin of Mohammed Baqir al-Sadr, one of whose daughters Muqtada married. Mohammed Sadiq al-Sadr was familiarly known as the "Second al-Sadr", drawing attention to his linkage to the militant stance of Mohammed Baqir al-Sadr and the latter's tragic

THE POST SADDAM ERA

death in 1980. He came to prominence in the 1990s, thanks to the support of the Baathist regime, which was always anxious to win supporters from among the clergy and, at the same time, was attempting to get religious backing for its policy of alliance with the tribal leaders. Since Mohammed Sadiq al-Sadr seemed relatively malleable and made a point of his Arab ethnicity, in contrast to the *marja'iyya*, which was monopolised by the Iranian Ayatollahs, he seemed the perfect choice for the Baathists. He proclaimed his *marja'iyya* and rapidly grew in popularity. In the end though, he turned against his Baathist patrons with various demands, including the right to give a sermon after the Friday prayer, a request unacceptable to the regime, since a sermon could provide the opportunity for mobilisation against the government, as had happened in the past. Mohammed Sadiq al-Sadr was therefore murdered in 1999, together with all his sons except for Muqtada, the youngest.

The moment Saddam Hussein was overthrown in April 2003, the young Muqtada made a thunderous entry on to the Iraqi political stage, using his embryonic militia to take control of a large Shia popular quarter in Baghdad, which he re-named Madinat al-Sadr: literally, Sadr City. Following this, he attacked all those who had collaborated with the former regime, especially those he called the "silent *marja'iyya*", in other words Ali al-Sistani, whom he accused of sanctioning through his silence the atrocities of the regime, and in particular the murders of Muqtada's own family. The initial stage in the escalation of violence came when Muqtada al-Sadr's supporters killed Abd al-Majid al-Khoei, the son of al-Sistani's predecessor, Abu al-Qasim al-Khoei, who had returned to Najaf after years of exile in London where he had headed an influential religious institution, the Khoei Foundation. Over the following days, the Sadrists surrounded the house of al-Sistani, whom they demanded should quit Iraq and return to Iran. Though al-Sistani had long been resident in Najaf, he had been born in Iran and still held Iranian nationality. In short, Muqtada al-Sadr took up a cause dear to his father, and incidentally also to the former Baathist regime: denouncing the Iranians who controlled the religious institution, he expressed his wish that Iraq should be for the Iraqis. In passing, he lost no chance to condemn the machinations of the Islamic Republic within Iraq.

Denouncing al-Daʻwa and SCIRI as Iranian agents, he also launched a more general onslaught on returnees from abroad. He condemned exiles, no matter where they came from, whose plan was to impose their will on Iraq with the assistance of the Americans, after fleeing from their country in a cowardly manner in the bad years instead of facing up to Saddam Hussein. In the same spirit, he called from the outset for the departure of the coalition troops, launching an insurrection against them in April 2004, while his militia, the Mahdi Army, attempted to gain control of Najaf. Muqtada al-Sadr lost the battle on the military front and was expelled from the Holy Cities, but despite American attempts to oust him he returned in strength to the political process some months later, gaining a foothold in Iraq's institutions. He forswore violence and entered the United Iraqi Alliance under two separate banners, the Sadr Bloc and the Virtue Party, which follows Ayatollah Mohammed al-Yaʻqubi, both a former associate and a rival of Muqtada al-Sadr, who now occupies a commanding position in southern Iraq. A third Sadrist faction, the Risaliyyin, which refused to participate in a list including the pro-Iranian SCIRI, fought the elections as part of a separate list. Overall, Sadrist factions took more seats than the other Shia movements. From that point on, the Mahdi Army gradually gained a foothold in the security forces, where its fighters were in direct competition with those of SCIRI's Badr Brigade. The two militias also fought each other, demonstrating yet again the overt hostility of Muqtada al-Sadr to any faction openly aligned with Teheran.

This brief overview of the complex phenomenon of the Sadrists demonstrates that, though his vision of the world is not far removed from that of many of the Iranian leaders, Muqtada and his supporters are in no way a pro-Iranian agency. Quite the contrary, the Sadrists are a phenomenon deeply rooted in the specificity of Iraqi Shiism as it had developed following the Gulf War of 1990–1991, during the years of sanctions that closed Iraq off from the outside world. It illustrates, furthermore, that the Arab and Iraqi nationalist ideology of the Baathist regime was not without impact on Shia society. As many see it, Mohammed Sadiq al-Sadr and his son Muqtada are products of Iraqi nationalism. In this context, what are we to make of interpretations that emphasise collusion between the Sadrists and Iran? Such analyses began to appear immediately after the visit of Muqtada al-Sadr to Iran in June 2003, during which he is said to have met a number of key figures in the Iranian regime, including Ayatollah Khamenei. The Pasdaran are said to have agreed at that time to take responsibility for training hundreds of Mahdi Army militiamen in camps in Iran and to begin to supply arms to the Sadrists. At the same time, Hezbollah is said to have received Sadrist fighters in its own training camps in Lebanon. In the south of Iraq, in particular, coalition forces also claim to have found Iranian weapons with the bodies of Sadrist militiamen killed in skirmishes. At the close of 2007, Muqtada al-Sadr established himself in the city of Qom, in Iran, where he spent three years completing his religious education and therefore enhancing his legitimacy in the eyes of his detractors, who had always tended to mock his poor religious credentials.

There is no doubt that there has been a rapprochement between Muqtada al-Sadr and the Islamic Republic, apparent, for example, from the much less aggressive nature of the young cleric's anti-Iranian rhetoric, to the extent that today it has virtually ceased. It is clear that he has grasped that in the present situation in Iraq, where the militias are still crucial, no Shia organisation can hope for influence without the support of Teheran. The rapprochement, however, is therefore certainly tactical and does not imply ideological or religious affinity. It is an alliance between players who have concluded that they depend on each other and that their interests may be mutual. Why would Iran support the Sadrists at a time when they were in increasingly violent conflict with the Badr Brigade, which was initially Iran's principal means of influence? The reason lies in Iran's realism and its pragmatism, together with its inclination not to put all its eggs in one basket. By playing off one side against the other, in other words by supporting a broad spread of Shia movements and even some Sunni guerrilla groups, Teheran ensures it is on the winning side in any situation. It is possible that this comprehensive approach may have offended its former favoured allies, and may indeed have been instrumental in SCIRI's decision to distance itself from Iran in 2007. Whatever the case may be, it serves as a further confirmation that Iran's foothold in Iraq is a result of the absence of a strong Iraqi central state, with its corollary of factional struggle for the control of resources and the absence of a monopoly over the exercise of force. It is not to be accounted for by existence of a transnational Shia community within which barriers between nationalities would wither away.

The reasons for conflict between Sunnis and Shias in Bahrain

Bahrain is another theatre where interpretation in terms of "regional" affinities has found expression since 2005. In late December 2005, a new development in Bahrain's always turbulent political life particularly seized the attention of various foreign newspapers and embassies. Mohammed Sanad, a cleric who up to then had taken little part in domestic political activity, was arrested at the airport, having, according to the authorities, incited rebellion against the regime in a sermon he gave some weeks earlier. His arrest sparked off an animated riot after several hundred people hastened to the airport to offer him their support, of whom ten or so were arrested and sentenced some months later to terms of imprisonment of up to two years. Bahraini government circles sent out the message that Mohammed Sanad was yet another agent sent by Teheran to destabilise Bahrain. Some even accused him of suggesting in his sermon that a popular referendum should be held in Bahrain about whether or not Bahrain should be linked to Iran. In short, for the Bahraini authorities, the incident provided tangible proof of Iran's hegemonic ambitions in the region. Another consideration was that Mohammed Sanad had for some years lived at Qom and had only occasionally visited Bahrain. He had been arrested as he stepped off a plane that had brought him back from Iran, which for the authorities was a further proof that he was an agent of Iran. The rioting at the airport and the agitation for his release, which was granted after only a few days, was seen as an indication of the extent of Iran's powerful connections in the local Shia population.

The version of events given by the authorities and passed on by the international press accords fully with the tendency, predominant after 2005, to interpret Shia political mobilisations in terms of regional tensions, and in particular in terms of Iranian power. In the case of Bahrain, however, such an interpretation does not hold up for long in the face of a closer examination of the facts, allowing them to be placed in a political context appropriate to the country itself. Mohammed Sanad was certainly a religious scholar who had for a very long time had his residence in Qom, where he had received his education, as had the majority of the clergy after the decline of the seminaries of Najaf. In Qom, however, he was well known as having been for a time an associate of Mohammed al-Shirazi, whose entourage he left to join the office of the *marja'* Jawad Tabrizi (who died in 2006), who exercised some influence in the Gulf monarchies. Relations between the Shirazists and the Iranian regime had been hostile, to say the least, for some twenty-five years, as has already been explained above. Ayatollah Tabrizi had never been an explicit opponent of the Islamic Republic, but was a *marja'* well known for his opposition to the doctrine of *wilayat al-faqih* and was entirely independent of state funds.

Though Mohammed Sanad had admittedly lived at Qom for many years, he was still not an Iranian agent. As to the statements threatening state security he had allegedly made in Bahrain, these were in fact totally innocent of any demand for the annexation of the country to Iran. In fact, Mohammed Sanad had simply lent his support to a petition launched some weeks earlier by a local opposition movement, al-Haqq (The Right), asking for a popular referendum on the new constitution promulgated in 2002 by King Hamad bin Isa Al Khalifa. The abrogation of this constitution was a constant theme of the opposition in Bahrain, which regarded this new version as worse than the constitution adopted by parliament in 1973, because it ruled out all possibilities of the establishment of a democratic regime. This view was shared by all the opposition movements, both Shia Islamic activists and liberals,[5] who were in cooperation on this issue. Al-Haqq had the intention of bringing its petition once more to the attention of the United Nations, which it had already tried some months previously, with little result. On that occasion, al-Haqq had asked the United Nations to lend its patronage to its demand for a referendum. It had also drawn the attention of the UN to the organisation's past role in relation to the same issue at the time of the consultation it had carried out in 1971 to gauge popular opinion on the question of Bahraini independence, when Bahrain was the object of a territorial claim on the part of the Shah of Iran. There was no question, therefore, of repeating the consultation of 1973. The intention was simply to remind the United Nations of its former involvement in order to encourage it to take a renewed interest in Bahrain, that would facilitate the internationalisation of the country's political crisis.

In view of all this, the conclusion is unavoidable: what Mohammed Sanad had done was merely to make an intervention in a political debate that had been running in his country for five years. It is true that he had spent much of his life in Qom, but he was in no way a supporter of the Iranian regime. In addition, he had never played an active role in any political party, and gave the appearance of being a person who did not wish to be involved in politics. Only the crisis that prevailed in his country had led him to intervene in the controversy.

For the Bahraini government, blaming Iran's apparently expansionist policies for the repeated occurrence of crises in the country meant it could avoid facing up to a number of problems. These related in part to the circumstances in which the state of Bahrain had been founded in the eighteenth century, and in part to the consequences of the collapse of Bahrain's welfare state system. As has been pointed out, the Al Khalifa dynasty that currently rules Bahrain was originally a Sunni tribal group from central Arabia. They conquered the archipelago that became Bahrain in the eighteenth century, when they subjected the local peasantry, who were Shias, to virtual serfdom. The social rift between conquerors and conquered has never been healed. Reforms were undertaken by the British in the 1920s that brought to an end the servitude of the Shia peasantry but brought no underlying change to the social hierarchy. Today, in a country where 70 per cent of the population is Shia, the Sunnis, who include both the ruling family and the allies who helped to conquer Bahrain, hold all the power in their hands.

In the state of disunity that prevails, the ruling dynasty has always regarded Bahrain's Shia population as a danger. Independence from British control in 1971 was the opportunity for an early exercise in democratisation that should have allowed the Shia population a voice in political decision making. A constituent assembly was installed in 1972, and in 1973, a parliament was elected under universal male suffrage. Marxist and Arab nationalist opposition parties predominated, followed by the Shia Islamic activists of al-Da'wa. A crisis soon followed when, in 1975, the Marxists, Arab nationalists and Shia Islamic activists allied themselves in parliament to block an emergency law put forward by the government appointed by the Emir. Parliament was dissolved, the constitution was suspended and many opposition leaders were obliged to go into exile, after which the reinstatement of parliament and the constitution it enshrined became the main demand of opposition figures of all ideological colours. The regime came through the crisis of 1975 with relative impunity thanks to the oil boom. The "oil shock" of 1973, which caused a crisis in the West but brought an unprecedented influx of cash to the oil producing countries, allowed the regime to buy itself a respite with the widespread distribution of dividends from its profits, mainly in the form of well-paid public sector sinecures. In the early 1990s, however, the fall in the price of oil and the drying up of its own reserves in combination with an explosive population increase, substantially reduced the ability of the state to redistribute wealth. This undermined its principal source of legitimacy in the eyes of the Shia population. Real unemployment, as distinct from the officially quoted figure, may, according to some, have still been as high as 30 per cent in the years following 2000, and mainly affected the Shias.

It is in this context that one should view what the Bahrainis call the *intifada* (an Arabic word used to refer to an "uprising") that took place in the period from 1994 to 1999. While the regime claimed the rising was the work of Shia militants, such as Hezbollah, who were agents for Teheran, the actual course of events shows that there was a series of demonstrations by the unemployed demanding mitigation of their plight. Most of these were led by Ali Salman (born 1965), a young cleric who quickly came to the fore as the leader of the *intifada*. When Ali Salman was arrested in 1994, for the organisation of a small committee protesting against a plan for marathon runners in shorts to run through his village, a riot ensued. This local uprising, which sparked off the *intifada*, was not in support of a figure whose popularity was based on his fight for Islamic ethics or his links with Iran: it was simply a gesture of solidarity for his action on behalf of the unemployed.

Though Ali Salman was a cleric educated in Qom, he was in no way a typical pro-Iranian activist. His *marja'* was not Ali Khamenei but the senior cleric in Najaf, Abu al-Qasim al-Khoei, and then from 1992 Ali al-Sistani, al-Khoei's successor. He was certainly close to Isa Qasim, one of the founders of al-Da'wa in Bahrain. However, he was never an active member of that movement. When he was exiled in 1995, he opted not to go to Iran, despite that being Isa Qasim's country of residence, but went instead to London. There, he associated himself with the leadership of the Islamic Bahrain Freedom Movement, which included lay officials from al-Da'wa, though he held aloof from any formal association with that movement. After the accession to power of a new Emir, whose initial plan was the transformation of the country into a constitutional monarchy and the opening up of new possibilities of political participation, he returned to Bahrain in 2001. He set up al-Wifaq to provide a framework within which all the Shia opposition currents, including especially al-Da'wa, Hezbollah and the Shirazists, could work together, resolving their old disagreements. Everything in Ali Salman's career and policies confirms that he was a leader whose position was rooted in domestic socio-political concerns, in contrast to the previous generation who had become politically active within movements imported from Iraq. His explicit goal was the exclusion of factional quarrels based on external religious and political clashes.

It was in order to unite the opposition that, in 2002, Ali Salman went into an alliance with the "liberals", the heirs of the Marxist and Arab nationalist movements of the 1970s, at the moment when the new Emir, who had by now proclaimed himself King, finally promulgated a new constitution that limited the freedom of the parliament considerably. The regime's refusal to compromise on this issue, together with the failure of socio-economic conditions to improve, explains the deterioration of the political situation. In October 2002, four opposition movements, including al-Wifaq, boycotted the parliamentary elections. Though 2003 passed without incident, as the regime and the opposition eyed each other warily, the intensification in 2004 of the opposition campaign for the abrogation of the new constitution led to an authoritarian crackdown by the regime. This entailed various limitations on free speech and on the freedom of action of the opposition, with arrests and beatings, as well as legislative measures intended to restrict freedom of association and free expression.

In 2006, al-Wifaq agreed to take part in parliamentary elections. However, this was not, as has been suggested, due to the example of the large electoral turnout in Iraq, which had been given the blessing of Ayatollah Sistani.[6] Once again, the decision was made on the basis of purely domestic considerations. What prompted Ali Salman to persuade his followers to go to the polls was his conclusion that he could exercise no political influence whilst remaining outside the existing institutions, together with his apprehension of too great a deterioration in relations with the ruling dynasty. He had his way, with 72 per cent of Bahrainis exercising their votes, though the regime did not yield an inch over the issue of the powers of parliament. On the other hand, the situation cannot be said to have become less tense: in fact, the opposite was true. The campaign of 2006 was marked by numerous incidents of a more or less serious nature. One of these was the split that took place within al-Wifaq, with the foundation of al-Haqq, which brought together veteran members of the party whose aim had been to maintain the boycott on electoral participation while drawing the crisis to the attention of the international community. More serious was the sequence of events known as "Bandargate". In the spring of 2006, Saleh al-Bandar, a British citizen of Sudanese origin who was working in the Bahraini administration, made public a 200 page report which exposed, in alarming detail, a far-reaching plan hatched by leading members of the ruling Al Khalifa family to "improve the general situation of the Sunnis in Bahrain". The plan actually suggested a reduction in the proportion of Shias in the population, principally through the naturalisation of hundreds of Sunni foreign residents, as well as the exclusion of Shias from key institutions such as the armed forces, the police and the information services.[7] The report revealed nothing new, as the opposition had long been aware of manoeuvres of this kind, which they had condemned, but for the first time it provided documentary evidence to support the charges and gave the names of the persons implicated. Naturally, Saleh al-Bandar was immediately ordered to leave the country and the individuals named were unanimous in denying their involvement. "Bandargate", however, cast a dark shadow over the elections, all the more damning because the electoral process had been carried out with no credible foreign observers. An organisation representing the Democratic Party of the United States, the National Democratic Institute, had been expelled from the country some months earlier. The opposition suspected that the government had taken advantage of this to engage in electoral fraud in order to prevent al-Wifaq from obtaining a majority in parliament and from securing the position of Speaker of Parliament. One of the tactics involved would have been for Sunni mercenary employees of the armed forces and the security services, who had recently been granted Bahraini citizenship, to register their votes in mobile ballot boxes whose contents were attributed to regions where al-Wifaq's allies, a handful of liberals, most of them Sunnis, were liable to win. In fact, given the distribution of constituencies, which gave sparsely populated Sunni regions the same weight as heavily populated Shia areas, al-Wifaq could in any case only have hoped to win the speakership through an alliance with the liberals.

The participation of al-Wifaq in the 2006 elections did not, therefore, lead to the re-establishment of confidence between the opposition and the regime. By the close of 2007, the political situation in Bahrain was even more intractable, to the point where many observers were already not ruling out a further uprising in the country, which had become inured to such events. The concatenation[8] of revolts that hit the Arab world from December 2010 onward provided the spark that ignited this explosive situation. On 14 February 2011, people assembled in a number of Shia villages to express the kind of broad message associated with other such movements throughout the Arab world. Those involved were mostly young people not engaged in formal political organisations, and their demands were democracy and the improvement of socio-economic conditions. The regime's reaction was immediate and uncompromising, with the police killing and injuring several demonstrators. This, however, only emboldened the protestors, who were quickly joined by the formal opposition movements, with the Pearl Roundabout in Manama becoming the heart of yet another uprising. After failed attempts at dialogue between al-Wifaq and the reformist faction of the ruling family, this uprising was eventually suppressed on 18 March with the help of Saudi troops and forces from the UAE. At the time of writing, Bahrain was witnessing probably the most severe crackdown on opposition ever conducted by the Al Khalifa dynasty, with its share of arbitrary arrests, torture, intimidation and summary military justice. Something totally unprecedented occurred when some forty Shia shrines, mosques and cemeteries were vandalised and some of them destroyed, while, in some areas, Sunni public figures called for a boycott of Shia businesses. In other words, there was an explosion of sectarian tension in Bahrain, where there had seldom throughout history been clashes between Sunnis and Shias, in which the backing of Sunni sectarian movements by the regime's hardliners was certainly decisive.

THE POST SADDAM ERA

Unsurprisingly, the regime resorted to its familiar rhetoric to justify the crackdown in the eyes of its Western and regional allies, principally the United States, which has had a naval base in the country for more than sixty years. The protesters, the regime maintained, were not democrats but agents acting on behalf of Iran, a country whose atavistic expansionism was once more threatening to disrupt the regional status quo. While ignoring the appeals to Iran made by officials of al-Wifaq not to meddle in Bahrain's domestic affairs, the Bahraini authorities were quick to interpret comments by opposition leaders so as to serve their own version of the events. The most commented upon in this respect was a statement by Hassan Mshaima, the leader of al-Haqq, who declared to the Reuters news agency that he wanted a "republic" to replace the monarchical regime in his country. The Bahraini authorities were quick to rephrase the sentence in question to read as if Mshaima had called for the establishment of an "Islamic Republic", an objective which would not have been in line with Mshaima's career as a typical *effendi*, a lay Shia Islamic activists who had made no secret that his view was that the involvement of the clerics in politics was harmful.

However, while the Shia transnational connections played no role in initiating the Bahraini 2011 uprising, which was the combined result of accumulated domestic anger together with the regional context of the other Arab uprisings, they came into play after the intervention of the Saudi and UAE forces. They acted within the framework of the so-called "Peninsula Shield", a joint military force including soldiers from all the states of the Gulf Cooperation Council, where Saudi Arabia, as the GCC's leading country, has the upper hand. What most of the Shias saw as an unacceptable foreign intervention sparked international protest, both in the West and, significantly, among Shia religious and political leaders in the Middle East. The Iranian Ministry of Foreign Affairs issued an official communiqué condemning the move, triggering yet another diplomatic crisis with Bahrain and its GCC allies. Later on, Iranian activists chartered boats with "humanitarian aid" which sailed towards Bahrain and were, of course, rebuffed by GCC boats. Nuri al-Maliki, the Iraqi Prime Minister, also made declarations condemning the crackdown by the Bahraini authorities. For his part, Ali al-Sistani closed Najaf's seminaries for one day in protest. The Sadrists organised demonstrations, mainly in Baghdad, which gathered hundreds of people. In Lebanon, Hezbollah, which watched events in Bahrain closely and reported them through its various press organs, was also unrelenting in its criticism.

To date, little has resulted from this international Shia protest. It had no impact on events on the ground. Indeed, if anything it lent credence to the Bahraini regime's rhetoric about a Shia plot driven by Iran and, therefore, embarrassed those Bahraini Shia activists such as Ali Salman who were at pains to demonstrate that they had no link whatsoever to Teheran. Significantly, the transnational protest did not follow the outlines of the networks of Shia Islamic movements as they have been described in the previous chapters of this book. They were expressions of an amorphous religious solidarity rather than of an organised transnational network of activists. Moreover, they reflected the concern of important Shia political actors who, though unable and most probably also unwilling to impact the situation on the ground, nevertheless aimed to preserve or build an image of tutelary power for the Shias worldwide. This was clearly the case for the Islamic Republic of Iran, which felt it could not say or do anything while its Shia coreligionists were being violently suppressed just a few kilometres from its coasts, even though it should be said that Bahrain was no longer, if it had ever been, a priority within its policy of exercising influence. In other words, Iran has a reputation to keep up, which, even if it is increasingly overrated, still helps it to maintain its influence by giving the impression that it is stronger than it is in reality. All in all, the symbolic nature of the Shia transnational reaction to the crackdown on the Bahraini uprising confirms rather than contradicts the domestification of Shia political dynamics.

The Shias as supporters of the throne in Saudi Arabia

Saudi Arabia is certainly the country where the new regional disposition has had the strongest impact on the internal situation. This is particularly so in relation to the evolution of Shia political Islam, dominated in this case by the Shirazists. Here again, it is important that while there is a link between regional and domestic issues, it is domestic considerations that have been predominant. This process was actually initiated in the 1990s in the context of the liberalisation of the Saudi regime as the result of a conjuncture of economic and historical factors. On the one hand, while Saudi Arabia's geology still harbours the most extensive proven oil reserves in the world, the Saudi welfare state entered a crisis in the mid-1980s, following the collapse in oil prices and a growth in population. On the other hand, during the Iraq-Kuwait conflict of 1990–1991, the inability of the Saudi armed forces either to bring aid to the country's Kuwaiti ally or to protect the territory of the Kingdom itself from Iraqi incursions shook the Al Saud to the core. In addition, the appeal to non-Muslim foreign armies and the permanent installation of American forces on the soil of the Arabian Peninsula, the land of the divine revelation, further weakened the religious legitimacy of the dynasty and endangered its historic alliance with the Wahhabi *ulama*. The grand mufti Abd al-Aziz bin Baz, the Kingdom's supreme religious authority, was very close to the royal family and had issued a *fatwa* (a religious decree) sanctioning the recourse to foreign forces. However, as soon as Kuwait was liberated, he agreed to lend his support to a petition launched by a group of younger *ulama*, notably Salman al-Awda and Safar al-Hawali, who adhered to the ideas of the Muslim Brotherhood, calling on the Al Saud to pay more respect to Islamic values and to ensure their respect by others. The petition, soon followed by another, stressed the necessity for the Al Saud to embark on political reform in the country, with a wider distribution of power.

This challenge to authority, unprecedented in Saudi Arabia's history, came out of the heart of the institutions of Sunni orthodoxy, and especially from the religious universities that were abundantly funded by the regime. Therefore, as was to be expected, the Shia opposition formed no part of it. On the other hand, the Shias managed skilfully the royal family's changing perception of the implicit threat. Since before the Iraq-Kuwait war, the Shia cleric Hassan al-Saffar, had made discreet approaches to the Saudi regime. To indicate the change in his political agenda, he began by altering the name of his movement so that the erstwhile "Organisation for the Islamic Revolution in the Arabian Peninsula" (*Munazzama al-Thawra al-Islamiyya fi al-Jazira al-Arabiyya*) became the "Reform Movement" (*al-Haraka al-Islahiyya*). In the same spirit, publication of the movement's organ "The Islamic Revolution" was halted and a new magazine was issued under the title "The Arabian Peninsula", soon to be followed by others, including "The Oasis" and "The Word", whose content bore no relation to the revolutionary rhetoric of former years. In addition to the customary articles devoted to the history of the Shia regions of the Saudi Kingdom, whose objective was to counterbalance the official histories in which the Shia presence was totally ignored, there were now articles on such subjects as human rights, religious pluralism and loyalty to one's country. The message was clearly that pacific coexistence was possible, if the regime agreed to implement a certain number of reforms.

At the moment when the orthodox Sunni opposition abruptly emerged in 1991, the Reform Movement attempted at first to intensify its pressure on the regime by holding out the threat of an (un)holy union with the Sunni Islamic militants. The reaction was not long in coming. Returning to its former strategy of exploiting confessional divisions, the regime sought to disadvantage the Sunni opposition by offering a major reconciliation to the Shias, which it implemented in 1993 by allowing the return of some of the established leaders of the Shirazists, led by Hassan al-Saffar. Others, including Hamza al-Hassan, chose to remain in London in order to retain their freedom of speech, where they continue to publish a magazine and run an internet site,[9] which, though they do not always mince their words in relation to the Saudi regime, often contain a shrewd analysis of the Kingdom's political scene.

However, the return of the exiled Shia opposition did not lead to a fundamental change in the situation of the Shias within the Kingdom. Though the police were under orders not to interfere with Shia rituals, which were better tolerated than previously, discrimination of many kinds persisted throughout the 1990s. A similar situation prevailed in the religious sphere. The official educational curriculum still classified Shiism as a deviant doctrine. Obstacles to the construction of mosques and other places of worship remained in place. Shia religious courts, where personal matters were adjudicated, continued to lack proper state funding, as they had done since the foundation of the Kingdom in 1932. Worse, socio-economic discrimination also continued. Most significant in this respect was the displacement of Shias from most sections of the upper ranks of ARAMCO (the Arabian American Oil Company), which controlled the exploitation of oil resources. Traditionally, ARAMCO, based in the heart of the Shia region in eastern Saudi Arabia, had employed many Shias, for whom it had been an important vehicle for upward social mobility from the 1950s to the 1970s. Fears of subversion by revolutionary Shias within the Kingdom's economic powerhouse lay behind this policy. Henceforth, the Shias were in a minority position in ARAMCO, which many now scornfully took to calling GHAMIDCO, because of the large-scale recruitment of members of the al-Ghamid tribe, who came en masse from the south-west of the country to work in the oil industry and were given jobs at all levels within the company.

Since it had achieved a degree of reconciliation between the Shias and the regime, the situation of the Shia opposition on the eve of the events of 11 September 2001 had been in many ways normalised. However, because Hassan al-Saffar and his group had been unable to achieve the reforms they had hoped for, the opposition also remained deeply dissatisfied. Nevertheless, the tensions in the Saudi-US relationship caused by 11 September and the subsequent declaration by the United States of its intention to depose Saddam Hussein in Iraq gave the Shias back some strong cards. For the Saudi regime, a new kind of threat was emerging in which the Shias had a key role to play. The Bush administration had no desire for fundamental change in its alliance with the Al Saud but wanted to bring pressure to bear on them to undertake reforms necessary to stamp out the terrorist threat. Currency was therefore given by Washington to rumours of a partition of the Kingdom which would see the hiving off of the Eastern Province, the site of almost all the oil reserves, which was also the main centre of the Shia population. In this scenario, it was suggested that the Eastern Province could be attached to Bahrain, thus reconstituting the Shia entity of historic Bahrain (see Chapter 1), which was the aspiration of some Bahraini Shia Islamic activists and also, but to a lesser extent, of some Saudi Shias. In the wake of this, the rumour spread through Saudi Arabia, and soon through the entire Middle East, of a grand US-Shia alliance that would upset the balance of power in the region. The Americans, it was said, would first put the Shias in power in Baghdad, would then follow this with a reconciliation with Iran, and finally would grant the Shias of the Gulf their own state, thus giving them control over the largest oil reserves in the world.

It is very probable that, for the Bush administration, all this was never any more than a kite flown to alarm the Saudis. In

THE POST SADDAM ERA

that respect, the ploy succeeded, while, more broadly, American plans to remould the Middle East were seen by Saudi Arabia as the complete overthrow, to the detriment of the Saudis, of the regional order. In April 2003, once the demolition of the Iraqi regime was completed, events confirmed Saudi fears. Shia Islamic activists did indeed come to power in Baghdad. In addition, though the United States did not take the opportunity to settle its past differences with Iran, that with Saddam Hussein out of the picture, the Islamic Republic being able to interfere significantly in Iraq, would be the major beneficiary of the new American strategy in the Middle East. This was even before taking Lebanon into account, where another Shia force, Hezbollah, rose constantly in popularity in proportion to its "divine victories" over Israel.[10]

The unprecedented concessions the Al Saud granted to their Shia population, and in particular to the former revolutionaries led by Hassan al-Saffar, should be seen in this context. It must be said that Hassan al-Saffar and his associates yet again skilfully exploited the situation. When the rumours of the partition of the Kingdom and of a grand US-Shia alliance were at their peak, Hassan al-Saffar constantly reiterated his loyalty to the ruling dynasty, declaring that the Saudi Shias would never fall in with the plans of the Americans, which he condemned in the strongest terms. In his strategy of reconciliation with the royal family, he went as far as to condemn the 2004 report by the US State Department on religious freedom in Saudi Arabia, where there was specific criticism of the treatment accorded to Shias in the Kingdom, which he attacked as unacceptable interference in domestic Saudi affairs. His decision to support the regime over this issue did not fail to arouse misgivings amongst his entourage, some of whom felt his professions of fidelity to the Al Saud were excessive. However, they were repeatedly counterbalanced by statements much less supportive of the royal family. For example, in February 2003, on the eve of the American intervention in Iraq, an article in the "Wall Street Journal" became the talk of Saudi Arabia. The journalist reported statements by several of Hassan al-Saffar's circle to the effect that, "If separation means that we will get our rights, then of course we'd want it. But if the Shiites become partners, our problem can be resolved locally—without waiting for changes imposed from the outside".[11] The message was clear: the Shias were ready to support the Al Saud against pressures from outside, but only if their claims were met. Some weeks later, shortly after the fall of Saddam Hussein, Hassan al-Saffar and his group launched a petition under the title "Partners in the Nation", signed by some 450 Shia personalities of all political persuasions and all walks of society. The signatories professed unequivocal loyalty to the royal family, asking in exchange for the recognition of the Shias as being a legitimate school of religious law,[12] thus benefiting from the same rights as their Sunni coreligionists.

In a historic gesture, Crown Prince Abdallah[13] publicly received some of the petitioners, including Hassan al-Saffar himself. Some weeks later, he convened the first in a series of conferences described as a "national dialogue", devoted to dialogue between the different Islamic currents represented in Saudi Arabia. For the first time, Shia *ulama* sat in formal dress alongside their Sunni counterparts. The regime had finally recognised the Kingdom's religious pluralism. In 2005, two years later, the first municipal elections in half a century allowed the Shias once more to demonstrate their ability to mobilise, when, in an election where the overall turnout was low, they went to the polls in larger numbers than the Sunnis. A member of Hassan al-Saffar's circle, Ja'far al-Shayeb, was elected mayor of Qatif. At the same time, the number of Shias in the Consultative Council (*Majlis al-Shura*), a body appointed by the King in 1992, increased from two to four. In terms of demands for equality, some issues that had been held in suspense for years were at last dealt with. For one thing, administrative obstacles to the construction of Shia mosques, though not entirely removed, were agreed to have become less onerous than before. Also, the Shia religious courts were at last reformed, with the number of judges raised from two to seven. A court of appeal was set up in Qatif and another at Hufuf, in the governorate of Hasa. These appointments offered an opportunity to send signals of reconciliation to Hezbollah, both in Hijaz and in Iran, since the person appointed in 2006 as head of the Shia court of appeal in Qatif was Ghalib al-Hammad, a well-known figure reputedly close to Hezbollah in the Hejaz, who had lived for many years in Qom.

Changes in the regional situation therefore had a decisive impact on the status of the Shias in Saudi Arabia, even though the greatest task remained: namely to resolve the thorny problem of discrimination in the field of employment in a situation where competition for the best paid and least demanding sinecures in the public sector was fierce. It was significant, however, that regional dynamics did not "regionalise" the Shia question in Saudi Arabia, as had been the case in the immediate aftermath of the Islamic Revolution, in fact the reverse had been true. The situation had been managed on a strictly domestic basis. In the light of the Saudi regime's fear, skilfully manipulated by Hassan al-Saffar, of a linkage between the various Shia issues, the Saudi regime began to express its response in terms of the ideal of the nation. This new rhetoric was particularly articulated by King Abdallah and his entourage, who embarked on a reconstruction, tentative but nevertheless real, of the ideas concerning the nation's collective identity that had been promoted by the Al Saud ever since they first came to power. In place of religious homogeneity under the leadership of the Wahhabi *ulama*, which had never in reality been achieved, they substituted a plan for peaceful coexistence between the different religious components of the country.

Quite apart from the difficulties of implementing such a well-meant project, it should be said that it was never endorsed by some influential centres of power in the kingdom. In Saudi Arabia the King is in reality only *primus inter pares* and rules with the consensus of a coalition of princes, each of whom has his own administrative, regional, military or media fiefdom, as well as sometimes also seeking international support. King Abdullah is not a member of the faction which has been most powerful since the 1970s, the group of seven princes known as the "Sudayris". These are all the sons of Hassa bint Ahmad al-Sudayri, one of the many wives of King Abd al-Aziz, the founder of the Saudi state. Since Abdallah came to the throne, the Sudayris have worked to enlarge their networks and fiefdoms in the country in order to secure the succession for one of their members. The relative empowerment of the Shias should be seen also in this context. In his rivalry with the Sudayris, King Abdallah has endeavoured to enlarge his constituency, notably by appealing to marginalised categories of the population to whom he has presented an image of himself as a reformer, in a departure from his previous reputation as one of the most conservative and religious-minded of the great princes. However, the involvement of the Shias in Saudi royal factionalism has proved a mixed blessing. Perceived by the Sudayris as supporters of the King, the Shias suffered setbacks as the competition for succession intensified in 2008 and 2009, at a time when Crown Prince Sultan bin Abd al-Aziz Al Saud, aged 80 and suffering from terminal cancer, was widely expected to die imminently. In March 2009, emboldened by the King's benevolence, a group of young Shias performed a pilgrimage to the tomb of the Imams at the Baqi' cemetery in Medina. Such practices are considered impious by Wahhabism, however, and they were beaten by the religious police and taken into custody. The King attempted to have them freed, but was opposed by Prince Nayef bin Abd al-Aziz Al Saud, the powerful Minister of the Interior who is also the leader of the Sudayri faction and has ambitions to be the next King. The pilgrims were not released until Nayef himself intervened, in an act intended as a demonstration to the King of the limits of his power.[14] A few days later, Nayef was appointed deputy prime minister, a position that, according to an established tradition, entitled him to be the next crown prince. He was actually appointed to this position in November 2011 after the death of Sultan.

Most Saudi Shia activists today understand that the situation of their coreligionists is dependent upon a set of interlinked international and domestic factors with which they must deal as adroitly as possible. This explains why the Bahraini uprising did not spread to the Eastern province of the Kingdom. In fact, in February 2011, when Bahrain was in turmoil, there were some demonstrations by Saudi Shias. Significantly however, they failed to attract more than a few hundred people, mostly young people of unidentified political affiliation, who made no demand for democracy or freedom but asked for the release of political prisoners. This, they eventually obtained in many cases, including the release of a cleric named Tawfiq al-Amer who had expressed a wish to see the introduction of a constitutional monarchy. Meanwhile, Hassan al-Saffar and his aides had attempted to dissuade the "young men" (as they described them) from emulating the demonstrations in Bahrain, a move they considered would be highly detrimental to their existing strategy of negotiating improvements step by step while at the same time pledging loyalty to the dynasty. Together with the episode of the Baqi' cemetery in 2009, this demonstrates that relations between Saudi Shias and the regime will in future depend to a great extent on developments in the rivalry between the different royal factions, as well as on the capacity of Hassan al-Saffar and the Shia mainstream to maintain calm amongst those who favour a more radical type of action, who are mainly drawn from the economically disadvantaged young.

Lebanon: The stumbling block for the dynamic of domestification?

For a long time Lebanon was the arena of choice where the various crises of the region would merge and interact, which is what Iraq has become today. The civil war of 1975 to 1989 was the most striking instance of this phenomenon. Often described as a "proxy war", it was both an expression of the local crisis of the Lebanese political and economic model, and an opportunity for regional powers to settle their accounts with each other through the vehicle of the Lebanese militias. As has been seen, the civil war was the direct cause of the emergence of Hezbollah. Hezbollah was a jihadist movement that prioritised resistance against Israel, but was by the same token a means for Iran to position itself as a key participant in the conflict between Israel and the Palestinians, and more generally to assert itself as a regional power. In the field of opposition to Israel, Hezbollah eliminated all its potential rivals in Lebanon, including the Palestinian movements, the secular Lebanese parties and, of course, the Lebanese army itself, which was sidelined as the central state faded from view amidst the clash of the rival militias. From the 1980s, Hezbollah succeeded in monopolising resistance to Israel and the legitimacy that accrued from it. The end of the civil war in 1989 changed nothing. The Taif accords, which ended the war, provided for the disarmament of all the militias, but this was never implemented in the case of Hezbollah, which was able to argue that since Israel continued to occupy southern Lebanon it was excused from compliance. With Hezbollah disarmed, they asked, who would continue the struggle against the occupier and salvage the honour of the nation?

In 2000, the unilateral Israeli withdrawal from southern Lebanon re-opened debate on the case for the disarmament of Hezbollah, bringing the party face to face with its "first true strategic dilemma".[15] As there was no further scope for resistance against the Israeli occupation, Hezbollah should have relinquished to the Lebanese army the monopoly over the legitimate exercise of force. The difficulty was that no-one would seriously contemplate the risk of a violent confrontation with Hezbollah in order to disarm the movement, if it was unwilling to do it of its own accord. In practice, the dispute over the Shebaa farms served as an excuse for both parties to duck the issue. The Israeli army had not withdrawn from this small patch of territory at the junction of the Lebanese, Syrian and Israeli frontiers, which in its view was not Lebanese territory since it had been overrun by Israel in the course of driving out the Syrian army during the 1967 war. Israel though that this issue could only be settled in the context of negotiations with Syria, and not with Lebanon. The Lebanese government, on the other hand, as well as Hezbollah, regarded the question as one concerning Lebanese territory. The Syrian leadership concurred with this position, but refrained from making a clear statement on the matter to the United Nations. Whatever the truth was, the Shebaa farms gave Hezbollah the perfect pretext to continue the struggle for Lebanese sovereignty and thus to justify its refusal to disarm.

The emphasis Hezbollah placed on its status as a resistance movement accounts for the difficulties of its transformation into a conventional political party within the framework of the return to normal political life after the end of the Lebanese civil war. In this respect, it can be compared to Amal. Amal was the outcome of the transformation of the Movement of the Deprived into a militia after the start of the war, and had little difficulty in returning to civilian life. Its transformation was simplified by the fact that it had been militarily vanquished by Hezbollah during the inter-Shia confrontations that took place in the closing years of the war. Not only was a return to the political sphere its only remaining option, but it was also in accord with the movement's underlying tendency since its creation. Musa al-Sadr had struggled for better representation for the Shias in relation to the other religious communities, especially the Maronites and the Sunnis. It was more generally part of a process of social emancipation in which the political empowerment of the Shias would be strengthened by their greater integration into the apparatus of the Lebanese state. Today, Amal's power of mobilisation depends on its ability to offer access to public resources through the exercise of clientelism.

Hezbollah, on the other hand, operates in an entirely contrary fashion. It does not seek incorporation into the Lebanese state, putting itself forward instead as an alternative state. It has military resources which, if not equivalent to the Lebanese army, are at least sufficient to enable it to take on the army in the event of open conflict. In addition, it provides a wide variety of social services to the Shia population, including even the provision of running water in some villages in southern Lebanon and in some areas of south Beirut. This has all been achievable because of Hezbollah's access to sources of finance other than those of the state, with funds drawn from Iran, admittedly, but also from many contributors from within Lebanon, from the Lebanese diaspora and from the Gulf countries. In the TV station al-Manar, broadcast throughout the Middle East, Hezbollah also has at its disposal a highly effective means of communication, which is entirely independent of the Lebanese state.

The differing relationships of Amal and Hezbollah with the Lebanese state have resulted in an end to the division of labour, which was gradually adopted after the civil war. In addition to its role in the resistance, Hezbollah concentrates on local affairs. Meanwhile, Amal operates at the national level, for instance seeking representation in parliament where, from 1992, Nabih Berri has been the Speaker of Parliament. It also seeks ministerial posts and key administrative positions. In this field, it has agreed to represent the interests of Hezbollah.

Though the motivation of Hezbollah continues to be the goal of constituting itself as an alternative state, most observers agree that since the end of the civil war it has also sought a rapprochement with the institutions of the Lebanese state, to the extent that it has begun to use the expression "Lebanisation". Hidden within its self-presentation as a movement of resistance to the Israeli occupation, there lies the seed of an idea of national unity.

THE POST SADDAM ERA

In Hezbollah's own rhetoric, what it is defending is first and foremost Lebanese territory. In addition, from 1992, Hezbollah has opted to participate in parliamentary elections. As a result, it has regularly won eight or nine of the twenty-seven parliamentary seats reserved for the Shia community.[16] Thanks to its alliances, and particularly that with Amal, the parliamentary group of Hezbollah and its allies is usually the largest. Electoral participation itself implies conformity with the dominant conventions of Lebanese political life, which are characterised by clientelism and inter-communal negotiation. Hezbollah's charitable activities have certainly been an important factor in its electoral success, since they have enabled it to build wide networks of "clients". Hezbollah's clients are for the most part Shias, but significantly, others are from a variety of religious communities, including Christians of different denominations.

This is largely a result of the idiosyncratic nature of the Lebanese electoral system. In order to counterbalance the religious polarisation that is implicit in the quota system, and to promote negotiations between the communities, the framers of the constitution also incorporated the principal of territorial representation, which has the effect that every candidate must seek simultaneously to represent his community and his constituency, while the constituencies are in principle multi-confessional. The practical consequence is that, in order to be elected, a Shia candidate must be supported by the Shias but is obliged also to seek the support, for example, of the Christian voters in his constituency. For Hezbollah, this means that it must not only extend its welfare provision to other communities, but must also give guarantees of its observance of the so-called National Pact of 1943 between the communities (see Chapter 2). In short, participation in the elections implies the acceptance, in practice if not in theory, of the terms of the National Pact.

At first, the crisis that broke out in Lebanon in 2005, and has continued to the present day, worked in favour of the process of

Lebanisation within Hezbollah, but it also exposed its limitations. To look at the issue in context, 14 February 2005 saw the murder of Rafiq al-Hariri (1944–2005), who had since 1992 almost continuously occupied the position of prime minister and was the all-powerful leader of the Sunni community. Al-Hariri was assassinated by means of a car bomb, an attack most probably ordered by Syria, in which the Special Tribunal for Lebanon, set up by the United Nations in 2007 to investigate the case, suspects that Hezbollah was instrumental. This was Syria's response to al-Hariri's change of direction some months earlier when he spoke out against the extension of President Emile Lahoud's term of office at the behest of Damascus, without whose agreement no decision of importance could be taken in Lebanon, which had been occupied by the Syrian army since 1976. As prime minister, Rafiq al-Hariri took the view that the extension of Emile Lahoud's presidency was unconstitutional and also tipped the balance in favour of one of his great political rivals.

In the face of Syria's diktat, al-Hariri sought to internationalise the crisis by looking for support abroad, especially from France, where he was a personal friend of the French president Jacques Chirac. The affair ended up at the United Nations, where the Security Council passed resolution 1559, sponsored both by France and the United States, which called on Syria to withdraw from Lebanon and Hezbollah to lay down its arms. The following day, disregarding the resolution, Syria presided over the extension of Emil Lahoud's term of office, passed by a parliament where Syria's supporters were in a majority. Some days later, Rafiq al-Hariri resigned as prime minister, a move which placed him definitively in the anti-Syrian camp, taking with him the majority of the Sunni community, who had been the traditional agents of Syria's influence in the country since its creation. While the anti-Syrian camp had always been a minority within Lebanon's political class, they suddenly found themselves in a position of strength.

THE POST SADDAM ERA

Rafiq al-Hariri's assassination was Syria's logical response to this development, but it provoked an unprecedented popular protest movement that rapidly came to be known as "the Cedar Revolution". The high point of this was the anti-Syrian demonstration of 14 March 2005, which was the largest ever gathering in Lebanon's history, with more than a million people, and led to the foundation of the multi-confessional political grouping known as the "March 14 Alliance", whose watchword was the independence of Lebanon. Syria did not insist on having its way and in April 2005 withdrew its troops, but continued to harass Lebanon with a campaign of targeted assassinations of leading figures in the anti-Syrian movement.

In this crisis, where have the Shias positioned themselves, and what was the attitude of Hezbollah, which is their principal representative? Since the Syrian intervention in Lebanon in 1976, the Shia movements had been some of Syria's leading allies. The relationship between Syria and Hezbollah is basically of a tactical nature, despite the fact that a religious alliance has often been spoken of, drawing attention to the dominant role of the Alawites in the Syrian regime. Before the passage of resolution 1559, Hezbollah was a useful instrument for Syria to keep up the pressure on Israel. For Hezbollah, Syria's support was vital, since the flow of arms donated to Hezbollah by Iran passed through the territory of Syria, Iran's long-standing ally. By linking the issues of Syrian withdrawal and the disarmament of Hezbollah, resolution 1559 only served to bring Syria and Hezbollah somewhat closer. The Sunni move into the anti-Syrian camp left Hezbollah and its ally Amal virtually alone in the pro-Syrian group. The notorious demonstration of 14 March had in fact been a response to a demonstration on 8 March which had rallied 800,000 people to "say thank you" to Syria. Nevertheless, Hezbollah remains wary of Syria and has no desire for the restoration of its hegemony over Lebanon. For the moment, however, Syria's backing for Hezbollah is a simple necessity for it to maintain its military strength and thus to perpetuate the myth of "resistance", which is the pillar of its political legitimacy. In this context, Hezbollah seeks external support in order to maintain its internal integrity, in a tactic characteristic of other Lebanese groupings.

While the shake-up in political alignments has prompted Hezbollah to strengthen its alliance with Syria, however, it has also obliged it to seek closer ties with the Lebanese state. This was shown by the parliamentary elections of 2005, after which Hezbollah opted for the first time in its history to take part in a coalition government with anti-Syrian groups, thus accepting full participation in the interplay of compromises and alliances that have always characterised Lebanese political life. The signature in 2006 of a memorandum of understanding with the Free Patriotic Movement of the Maronite leader Michel Aoun, long the champion of the fight against the Syrian presence in Lebanon, is another sign of Hezbollah's adaptive capacity. So also is its decision to participate once more in the government in the framework of the national unity government established after the much disputed 2009 elections. Too much should not be made of this, however, since, in both instances of its participation in government, Hezbollah had no governmental plans beyond blocking any suggestion that the government might enact the UN's injunction to disarm the militias or to indict its officials for the assassination of Rafiq al-Hariri. Hence, even while it was an element in the 2005 government, it did not neglect to fan the flames over the Shebaa farms conflict, carrying out further operations against Israel that enabled it to maintain its identity as a resistance movement and to demonstrate its determination not to be disarmed. In July 2006, it was one of these operations that sparked off the war with Israel, with dramatic consequences for the civilian infrastructure in Lebanon. For Israel, the participation of Hezbollah within the Lebanese government offered a justification for its decision to lay waste the entire country in response to Hezbollah's pinpricks on the frontier. The argument was that since Hezbollah was an element in the government, then the government must have endorsed Hezbollah's military operations. The objective was clearly to drive a wedge between Hezbollah and the Lebanese people and obtain measures of retaliation against it on the part of the government. This was a real misunderstanding of the exigencies of the Lebanese political process and especially of the weakness of the Lebanese state in relation to the "Hezbollah state".[17] The parties within the "March 14 Alliance" grasped the occasion of the massive destruction to condemn the deleterious role of Hezbollah and emphasise once more the need to disarm it. However, they still did not have at their disposal the means to carry out such a plan.

The war of 2006 also drew attention once more to Hezbollah's links with regional powers, this time not so much with Syria as with Iran, seen as the major beneficiary of the war. This conclusion was drawn both by observers and by the regimes of the region, and especially those that were hostile to Iran, such as Saudi Arabia, Jordan and Egypt. The timing of the kidnap of the two Israeli soldiers on the Lebanese border on 12 July 2006 coincided perfectly with a delicate moment in the negotiations between Iran and the international community over its nuclear programme, which is suspected of having military intent. From Iran's standpoint, increasing the tension in the Middle East through the medium of its old ally was a convenient way of distracting attention, while also making a further demonstration of its ability to act outside its frontiers. Iranian interest in the kidnap, however, does not mean it was commissioned by Iran, and on the basis of current information, it is impossible to say for certain that Hezbollah was doing Teheran's bidding. A further issue is that though a response from Israel was to be expected it was unlikely that the scale of the retaliation could have been anticipated. Hezbollah no doubt saw the kidnap as just another guerrilla operation which would in any case have no major consequences and might well enhance its prestige in Lebanon and in the Arab and Muslim world, where the struggle against Israel is a source of legitimacy always easy to activate. In addition, while the war led the Shias to close ranks behind Hezbollah, to the extent that they felt themselves attacked as a community, all the signs were that the Shia population, the first victims of the war, had not wished to see Hezbollah involve itself in any new resistance operation. The Shia community sometimes even appeared critical of Hezbollah's adventurism and only appeared to back resistance when it took the form of deterrence, which is the line that Hezbollah has in any case taken since the Israeli withdrawal in 2000, from which it is difficult to say whether the operation of 2006 was a real deviation.

What is certain, however, is that the war of 2006 reinforced the strategic importance of Iran's relationship with Hezbollah. Not only did Hezbollah need to replenish its stock of arms, destroyed in the Israeli attacks, it was also only able to play its part in the reconstruction effort by calling on subventions from Teheran. Certainly, in this field, other generous donors came forward, but the powerful Iranian religious foundations, directly under the control of the Guide, Ali Khamenei, continued to predominate. Nevertheless, Hezbollah made no change in its internal policy within Lebanon, demonstrating its concern to maintain its relations with the other communities and avoiding any new rise in tension. Hezbollah was conscious that confessional polarisation had intensified after the war, and was aware that in the context of the continuing political crisis, and with the rearmament of the former militias, it could be precipitated into a new political crisis for which it had no more desire than the other factions did. In this sense, it is legitimate to speak of Hezbollah's quest for Lebanisation.

However, a false interpretation should not be put on this process. Lebanisation is taking place, in the sense that Hezbollah has been assimilated into the political culture of Lebanon, and has accepted the principle of the indispensability of the National

Pact between the communities. On the other hand, it would be incorrect to speak of Lebanisation in the sense of integration into the Lebanese state. For the moment, Hezbollah remains in an external relationship to the state, and participates only in order to avoid state interference, not to take the state over. This is a major difference from the situation in the Gulf monarchies and in Iraq. Owing to their providential possession of oil wealth, the Gulf states have acquired a considerable power of attraction over political actors and civil society. In Iraq, weak and vacillating though it may be, the state is nevertheless the principal prize of political struggles. The various movements and militias, both Shias and others, seek to achieve influence within it or to control it entirely. In Lebanon, by contrast, the state is not seen by Hezbollah as the main prize. Its preferred objective is to maintain itself as an alternative state, keeping the Lebanese state at arm's length while establishing a modus vivendi with it. This is not altogether a conscious strategy on the part of Hezbollah. It also results from the inability of the Lebanese state to impose its authority and, frankly, its lack of attraction for a major Shia party such as Hezbollah. Why, after all, should Hezbollah forgo its position of power in order to submerge itself in a state whose institutions were frankly conceived to give preference to the Maronite and Sunni communities? In other words, for the Lebanisation of Hezbollah to be fulfilled, the political institutions of Lebanon would need to be transformed in such a way as to take into account the interests of the Shia community, today the largest in numbers. The provisions of the National Pact would need to be revised, which would require a reorganisation of the confessional system or its complete abolition. In this process, Hezbollah is only one actor among others, and there is nothing to indicate that the Maronite and Sunni representatives would be ready to make any such concession, much less to be forced into it under duress.

CONCLUSION

TOWARDS THE SECULARISATION OF SHIA POLITICAL ISLAM

Examination of the various Shia movements in their respective national contexts indicates that they are predominantly motivated by domestic considerations, so that one could speak of a definite drift towards autonomy from the traditional centres of power constituted by Iraq and Iran. Autonomy, of course, does not signify merely the decoupling of political questions and absorption by states. In my view, it is also a manifestation of a wider phenomenon, namely that of the autonomy of politics in relation to religious authority. While most Shia political dynamics originated in Iraq and Iran, spreading into the neighbouring countries during the twentieth century, this was due to these two countries having become, as the result of a specific historical process, centres of religious authority in relation to which the other regions of Shia population were relegated to peripheral status. At the present time, it is this relationship between the centre and the periphery that is actually in the process of change, producing a map of the Shia world that is increasingly multipolar and simultaneously reveals a distancing from religious authority, as an organising principle of political dynamics. In other words, with the assertion of their autonomy from the centres, Shia movements are affirming their autonomy from the institution of the *marja'iyya* in which they had their origins decades before. Thereafter, their progress towards autonomy is bound up with the process of secularisation, in the sense of the attenuation of the status of religion as an organising principle of society and, in this case, as a source determining the making of political decisions.

The gap widens between clerics and laymen

It is counter-intuitive to refer to the secularisation of Shia political Islam since this contradicts an indisputable empirical fact: in the majority of Shia groupings, decision-making roles are filled by clerics, a situation little changed since the early 1960s. In the preceding chapters of this book, we have on a number of occasions drawn attention to the tension, within and between movements, that has characterised the relationship between lay and clerical officials. Everything suggests that the division between *effendis* and *ulama*, present from the start, has grown more profound over the years and is one of the principal factors driving the current process of secularisation.

At present, there are two movements that may, in our view, be said to have achieved secularisation, by the simple fact that clerics no longer occupy the executive positions within them and that they seek no connection with the *marja'iyya*: these are al-Da'wa in Iraq and Amal in Lebanon. As we have seen, the secularisation of al-Da'wa was the result of a schism in the late 1980s between the lay and clerical officials, followed by the withdrawal of the *ulama* from political activity. For the most part, these latter are now engaged in religious careers, some as freelance preachers and other within Iranian institutions. The lay officials, on the other hand, have taken key roles in the new regime in Iraq. The secularisation of the Amal movement also resulted from a schism between *effendis* and *ulama* which took place after the death of Musa al-Sadr, when the clerics set up Islamic Amal, later to become part of Hezbollah. The "Party of God" drew in most of the clerics, with the result that today

CONCLUSION

ulama represent only a tiny minority within Amal (with, in 2007, only two members out of a political bureau of twenty members) and in any case occupy positions of less influence than the *effendis*. Amal no longer describes itself today as an "Islamic movement" but as a "movement of believers", where party members are not recruited on the basis of their religious credentials. The fact that neither al-Da'wa nor Amal now refer in their constitutions to a higher religious authority endorsing the conformity of their political programme and their activities with Islamic law is an indication that secularisation is not just a fact but is also enshrined in law. In other words, they have fully accomplished the autonomy of politics from religion.

The same processes that led to the secularisation of al-Da'wa and Amal are at work within other Shia movements in the region, though less visibly. For instance, in all the Gulf monarchies, where the Shia movements are led by clerics, internal decision-making has been to a great extent secularised, or is in the process of such a change. One factor in play here is that the *ulama* lead their movements in consultation with lay officials, whether officially, as is the case with al-Wifaq in Bahrain, or as the result of informal power relations, as happens within the National Islamic Alliance in Kuwait. The secretary general of al-Wifaq is elected by the party's general assembly and major decisions, such as the boycott of the elections in 2002, and the decision to take part in the polls in 2006, are also taken in consultation with the membership. The National Islamic Alliance does not have formal procedures for the allocation of executive posts, so that any individual's position is on the basis of his personal social standing. In this context, the secretary-general Hussein al-Ma'tuk, properly educated in Qom and entitled to wear the turban, wields less power than the *effendi* Adnan Abd al-Samad, who has no formal position but, in the electoral context, is able to mobilise support from many directions beyond Shia religious circles.

A further factor is that secularisation manifests itself in terms of the respect shown by party members towards the clerical profession. Though clerical status continues to enjoy great standing, it is increasingly seen as a restriction on the free exercise of political thought. For example, it is not unusual to meet party members who have been conventionally educated in the *hawza* who either refrain from wearing clerical dress or have quite simply abandoned it. Several personalities from the Reform Movement in Saudi Arabia are to be found among these laicised clerics. One such is Tawfiq al-Seif, one of the earliest co-activists of Hassan al-Saffar, who was educated alongside him in Najaf and Qom and was also a member of the circle established in Kuwait by Mohammed al-Shirazi in 1970. Though he wore the turban in the 1970s, he now goes bare-headed and has published many tracts and articles on political issues. Another significant example is that of Mohammed al-Mahfuz. Younger than al-Seif, and also a member of Hassan al-Saffar's circle, he never adopted clerical dress though he had studied for a long time at Qom in the 1980s. According to the convention in the Gulf, he indicates his status as a man of learning in the religious sciences by wearing a white head dress (*ghutra*), but without the black band (the '*aqal*) customarily worn to keep it in place. This custom, though still observed only by a minority among the Shias, is noticeably increasing. However, it is not a Shia innovation, but was initially introduced by Wahhabi *ulama* whose intention was to distinguish their dress from Bedouin practices that were deemed impious. Because it is characteristically worn by the Bedouin, the '*aqal* is regarded by the *ulama* as a symbol of deviation from Islamic practice.

The adoption of this symbolic characteristic of Wahhabism by some Shia men of religion could appear perverse but is in fact fully consonant with the message they wish to convey. As Mohammed al-Mahfuz puts it, Islam can do without the *ulama* and may be regarded as a personal matter, between God and the individual believer, as the Sunnis believe. As has been seen, this

CONCLUSION

position is not new and had already been adopted by Ali Shariati in his day, but it is currently making a vigorous reappearance. No doubt, many view the distancing of an entire section of the Shia Islamic movement from the model of government by the clergy that prevails in Iran as part of a process of "Sunnification" of Shia political thought. This may indicate that the Iranian experience has in the end discredited the standing of the Shia religious professionals, or at least that doubt has been thrown on a particular style of practising the clerical profession.

Finally, secularisation finds expression in the concepts of political authority expressed by the Shia Islamic activists. In answer to the question why the Shia movements are most often led by clerics, they explain that this is not obligatory. In their view, clerics do not lead by virtue of their clerical status, but because of their activist experience and the extent of their political commitment. Such attitudes are exemplified by the positions expressed during the parliamentary elections of 2002 in Bahrain. The Shia opposition decided in the end to boycott the vote because parliament was not empowered to legislate independently of the power of the King. However, there was every indication that al-Wifaq's most influential clerical officials were in favour of participation and judged that the boycott could endanger a process of reconciliation with the regime that they thought should take priority at that stage of the process of liberalisation. The clerical officials involved were Ali Salman, the secretary-general, but also Isa Qasim, often described as al-Wifaq's "spiritual leader". Isa Qasim had no official link with the party and such influence as he exercised over its policies was the result of religious authority and of his moral ascendancy over Ali Salman. There is a furious internal debate, among the membership of al-Wifaq and others, between those who think Ali Salman's appropriate role was that of a figurehead with Isa Qasim having the last word, and others who believe that Isa Qasim's influence is limited.

Adopting the position customary among high-ranking *ulama*, Isa Qasim denies that he had any links with al-Wifaq and takes care never to appear as if he belongs to a party. The greatest discretion enveloped his connections with al-Wifaq and Ali Salman. However, it was incontestable that al-Wifaq's boycott of the elections of 2002, against the advice of the most influential clerics, was backed by the party's popular base, consisting mostly of younger men. Asked why they had taken the party in a direction contrary to that favoured by the religious hierarchy, these young members were quick to reply that in matters of politics, the opinion of a cleric, even of a *marja'*, does not outweigh that of an ordinary party member who is well informed and in full knowledge of the facts. The only special competence the members conceded to the clerics who led al-Wifaq, and especially to Ali Salman, whom the members respected for his role in the *intifada* of 1994–99, was that which they derived from their political experience. Religious scholarship was in itself insufficient. In addition, in explanation of their personal stance in relation to the boycott, the members offered a distinctly secular analysis of the relationship between politics and religion. There was certainly no separation in Islam, as they saw it, between the two domains, and there they were in perfect agreement with traditional doctrine. On the other hand, when a *marja'* exercises his powers of interpretation on political questions, he is entitled to pronounce only on broad generalities, such as, for instance, the legality of participation in an electoral process. However, should a *marja'* venture to offer advice on a concrete political situation, his opinion does not have the force of law and should be regarded as just another opinion, with no more validity than that of a layman.

The marja'iyya in politics

Far from being the product of some local particularity, the ideas expressed by the young activists of al-Wifaq actually reflect the canonical conception of the relationship between politics and

CONCLUSION

religion in today's Shia world, held by clergy as well as laymen. Another episode from Bahraini political life provides an example: the later decision by Ali Salman and other leading figures in al-Wifaq to participate in the elections of 2006. Aware that such a decision would not attract universal approval and that it would need to be endorsed by the party rank and file, they embarked in 2005 on a campaign to explain the reasons for their choice. Their arguments were couched at the level of tactics: since the boycott of 2002 had not led to any progress on the issue of the revocation of the constitution, while if anything the situation had deteriorated in the sphere of public liberties, an attempt had to be made to take action through participation in the existing institutions. The debate was particularly heated, but by the spring of 2006, Ali Salman had obtained a favourable vote from the membership. Meanwhile, those who wanted to continue the boycott had left al-Wifaq to join al-Haqq. Nevertheless, the population as a whole still had to be persuaded to vote and in this respect, the battle was far from won. It was in this context that some weeks before the elections al-Wifaq took the decision to seek the assistance of an ally of substance in the form of Ayatollah al-Sistani. Through the intermediary of their personal contacts in al-Sistani's office in Najaf, some of the party's officials succeeded in making contact by telephone with the son of the *marja'*, Mohammed Redha al-Sistani, who acted as a bridge between Ali al-Sistani and the public. Having consulted his father, he gave them his assurance that in the view of the *marja'*, al-Wifaq's decision to participate in the elections was correct. Some days later, in the course of a meeting with the membership, Ali Salman announced al-Sistani's opinion, and al-Wifaq circulated large quantities of leaflets making it known that there had been a *"fatwa"* from the master of Najaf supporting participation in the elections.

A preliminary conclusion can be drawn here, namely that al-Sistani's so-called *"fatwa"* was issued after the event to justify a political decision that had already been made internally by the party. The *marja'iyya*, therefore, had no role in the process of political decision-making. Equally significant were the debates that followed the announcement of al-Sistani's *"fatwa"*, which had an explosive effect in Bahrain, and in particular amongst those who supported the continuation of the boycott, who condemned what they said was a shameful and even scandalous manipulation of religion in a political affair. The arguments put forward were identical to those adduced by the rank and file members of al-Wifaq to justify the decision to oppose the advice of the clerics in 2002: namely that in practical political matters each person should follow his own conscience and that the view of the *marja'* did not have the force of religious law. Hassan Mshaima, the leader of the al-Haqq movement, within which those in favour of a continued boycott were now regrouped, suggested that the Shias were in the process of making the same mistake as the Christians, by attributing to their clerics an authority that in reality exceeded their competence. Mshaima, who had been a member of al-Da'wa in the 1970s, had not attended religious seminaries and claimed to possess self-taught religious knowledge, purporting to be more learned than many who were entitled to wear the turban. Indeed, he took the view that the "cult of the turban" represented a major peril to the faithful.

Hussein al-Najati was Ali al-Sistani's official representative in Bahrain. He was neither a member of al-Wifaq nor any other political party, and he generally remained aloof from political controversy. In the context of the mounting quarrel over the issue, he emerged from his seclusion to issue a statement setting out in detail the position of the *marja'* and in particular the status of his pronouncements. While it was true that Ali al-Sistani's view was that participation was the most "appropriate" (sic) course of action, he had not initially wished to make this known because it was simply counsel given on a private basis and not a *fatwa*, that is to say, a view that had the force of law. This coun-

CONCLUSION

sel was based on the diagnosis of a concrete political situation of which the *marja'* had after all only a limited knowledge as he was not resident in Bahrain. Henceforth, each person had the right to make their own diagnosis which would be of a value equal to that of the *marja'*, if not more so since Ali al-Sistani was perfectly aware that, as he put it, "those who have direct experience of the situation are aware of issues of which outsiders are ignorant".

This communiqué made it clear that the secularisation of politics was now a fait accompli, both for participants in political affairs and for the religious institution. This applied even to those clerics who, in contrast to Ayatollah al-Sistani, took an interventionist view of the relationship between politics and religion. A case in point was the position of the Shirazists. After Mohammed al-Shirazi died in 2001, he was succeeded by his brother Sadiq (born 1942), who still lived in Qom at the time of writing and has never returned to Iraq. Like his late brother, who retired from politics at the end of his life under pressure from the Iranian regime, Sadiq al-Shirazi refrained from expressing opinions concerning concrete political situations, especially in relation to the Gulf monarchies where he had his most faithful and wealthiest supporters. Like al-Sistani, he judged that intervention in political affairs through the issue of official communiqués would be beyond his authority, and moreover that this was not what his supporters wanted. In this respect, he gave complete latitude to his local representatives, whom he judged better informed than himself in relation to the actual situation. Meanwhile, he only commented on political issues in Iraq, regarding which he felt himself fully able to speak, since, even though he no longer lived there, Iraq was his country of origin, of whose concerns he regarded himself as having an intimate knowledge.

The only *marja'* who might continue to be at odds with this kind of interpretation of the relationship between politics and religion is Ali Khamenei. His official position would seem completely to contradict the notion that politics is the affair of those intimately concerned rather than others who may be at a distance. This is precisely because the *marja'iyya* which he claims relates to those at a distance from him rather than those close by: in other words not his fellow Iranians but to Shias resident outside Iran's frontiers. However, in practice Ali Khamenei's position is the same as that of the other *maraji'*. First, he refrains from public statements about the affairs of various countries where his coreligionists might be involved. Like al-Sistani, he voices his opinion only in the course of private conversations with activists from the various "Line of the Imam" movements. In the context of paranoia over supposed organic links between Iran and Shia communities, it should be said that this is a sensible line for the leader of a country which, despite its bid to become a regional power, is at the same time concerned to build better relations with its neighbours. Moreover, opinions given by Khamenei are expressed after the event, in relation to decisions already taken in private, or in any case are couched in terms sufficiently imprecise that activists are left to make the final decision for themselves. This has been the case with Hezbollah in Lebanon, for example. According to the movement's leaders, there have been up to now just two cases where Khamenei has been asked to pronounce on political decisions. First, in 1992, after the political bureau of the party had voted by an overwhelming majority to take part in parliamentary elections; and second, in 1998, before the party took the decision not to take part in the government. In the first case, Khamenei supported the decision to participate in the elections. In the second instance, his opinion had been sought because party officials were hesitant over the best course of action to take, but his reply had not been particularly helpful: in effect, Khamenei said, "Do whatever is in your best interests", in other words, they must do whatever they deemed best. Finally, it should be added that

CONCLUSION

beyond Lebanon, the positions adopted by activists who accept the *marja'iyya* of Ali Khamenei in relation to concrete political decisions are no different from those of others. They also take the view that the word of the *marja'* in reference to such cases does not have the force of law. To sum up, all the signs are that Ali Khamenei has been swept up by the movement towards the secularisation of politics.

The rise of millenarianism

As a social phenomenon progresses it often gives rise to contrary reactions, which, while indicating the outbreaks of resistance to which the phenomenon may have given rise, also serve as a measure of the vigour with which it is spreading. It is in this sense that the recent rise of millenarianism within the Shia Islamist movement must be understood. The messianic expectation of the return of the Mahdi, the twelfth Imam occulted by God from the view of men, who should make his appearance at the End of Days, has been a fundamental element of Shia doctrine since the ninth century. However, the rise to prominence of the clergy, together with the triumph of the rational ways of thought by which it has been accompanied, have rendered eschatological anticipation marginal to religious life. Over the course of history, outbreaks of millenarianism have been fiercely opposed by the clergy, who see them as threats to their monopoly of religious authority. This is a justified apprehension, since the advent of the Mahdi, or of some representative purporting to have had direct contact with him, would be nothing less than a sign of the termination of the intermediary function of the clergy. In addition, millenarian movements are often typified by a fierce anticlericalism. One of the most significant episodes of this kind was the suppression of the so-called "babist"[1] movement in Iran in the nineteenth century, orchestrated by the clergy, which in the end gave rise to the emergence of a new religion, Bahaism.

In the recent past, two political phenomena in the Shia world have been interpreted in terms of the resurgence of millenarianism, namely the emergence of the Sadrists in Iraq and the rise of President Mahmud Ahmadinejad in Iran. The writings of Mohammed Sadiq al-Sadr, Muqtada's father, were already characterised by a definite tendency towards millenarian prophecy. Millenarianism was part of his armoury as he sought to compensate for his lack of legitimacy, at the time when he was the *marja'* appointed by Saddam Hussein and faced the hostility of the establishment that surrounded Ali al-Sistani. His son, Muqtada, who also falls back on millenarian discourse, is in an even more difficult position than was his father in terms of religious legitimacy, since he cannot claim the status of *marja'*, nor even that of a *mujtahid* qualified to offer independent interpretation of religious texts. In contrast to what many predicted at the outset of his political career, however, the absence of religious legitimacy has not been a handicap for Muqtada since his movement, though fractured, is central to the political scene in Iraq today. This is yet another symptom of the advance of secularisation, since it shows that a political movement does not need the endorsement of the *marja'iyya* in order to succeed. As a necessary precaution to ward off criticism, however, al-Sadr has symbolically designated as his party's *marja'* Ayatollah Kadhem al-Ha'iri, a former member of al-Da'wa now based in Qom, who was a friend of his father from his student days. All agree, however, that the opinions of this *marja'*, who commands only a few followers in the Shia world, Iraq included, have little influence over the policies of the Sadrists. In reality, rather than officially placing himself under the authority of al-Ha'iri, Muqtada al-Sadr has turned the religious institution's hostility towards him to his advantage in consolidating his political power-base, representing better than anyone else the young disadvantaged Shias of the Baghdad slums who make up the specific social stratum from which he draws his support. These young Sadrists, themselves the victims of social deprivation and in search of recognition, regard Muqtada al-Sadr's shortcomings as a reflection of the prejudice they themselves suffer and as a sign of messianic designation. His marginality in relationship to the religious institution has made him the embodiment of their desire for revenge on an institution that they feel has abandoned them, and towards which their hostility is furious.[2]

As with Muqtada al-Sadr, recourse to the traditions of millenarianism as a means to gain legitimacy has been from the outset a stratagem of Iran's President Mahmud Ahmadinejad, as is shown by his repeated allusions to personal contact with the Mahdi. A particular instance came after his speech at the United Nations just months after his first election in 2005, when he reaffirmed Iran's right to pursue its nuclear programme. He averred that, at that precise moment, he had felt the presence of the Mahdi, which had given him strength to defend his position before a hostile international community. In addition, following his election, he has paid particular attention to the site of Jamkaran, to which he has given further government subventions. Only a few kilometres from Qom, Jamkaran is a little town where there is a mosque which, according to tradition, had been built on the orders of the Mahdi himself to await his return. Even before Ahmadinejad's rise to power, the government had lavished funds on the site, which became one of Iran's leading pilgrimage destinations. The faithful flocked there to throw scraps of paper, on which were written wishes that they hoped would be fulfilled, into a well. Ahmadinejad himself is said to have thrown a list of the names of his future cabinet into the well.

It is possible to discern motivations behind the attitude of the Iranian president similar to those at work in the case of Muqtada al-Sadr. Like Muqtada al-Sadr, Ahmadinejad lacked his own religious legitimacy, since he was no cleric but rather a layman with no history of attendance at religious seminaries. However, he enjoyed an electoral and popular legitimacy, which was sufficient for his position as long as he was able to put into effect the promises of economic well-being and social justice that had brought him to power. The dimension of populism was omnipresent in Ahmadinejad's public posture, which earned him the hostility of other Iranian politicians, who condemned him as a demagogue, as well as the antagonism of the religious institution, and of Ali Khamenei, the Guide of the Revolution. Khamenei is said to keep the reins of power in his own hands and, especially since Ahmadinejad's election, his role has been interpreted as a guarantee of the continuity of power in Iran and therefore of the country's foreign policy, which, despite the president's radical speeches at the United Nations, remains fundamentally little changed. In this sense, it could be said that Ahmadinejad and Khamenei are complementary, embodying respectively the popular and religious aspects of the legitimacy of the Islamic Republic. On the other hand, there is great tension in the relationship, of which the president's millenarian rhetoric is one expression. As with Muqtada al-Sadr and the *marja'iyya* of Najaf, its function is to bypass the authority of the Guide by making a direct appeal to a non-clerical religious legitimacy founded on direct contact with the divine. If the Mahdi speaks directly to Mahmud Ahmadinejad and inspires his policies, there is no need for a Guide to ensure that Iranian policy is in conformity with Islam. In such a situation, millenarianism is a form taken by the anticlericalism of lay Islamic officials.

The case of Mahmud Ahmadinejad, like that of Muqtada al-Sadr, leads us to the formulation of a final conclusion, less regarding what secularisation is than what it is not: it is not a form of moderation, in word or deed. In itself, secularisation is neither good nor bad, in the sense that it is not conducive to the elaboration of particularly optimistic scenarios for change. It is simply a fact that informs us about the imperatives of politics, viewed as practice in the real world, based on a permanent process of negotiation and compromise, which permits, by its very

CONCLUSION

nature, policy options that may be at variance with official and declared religious values. It also throws light on the necessity for the religious institution to maintain a certain distance from politics if it wishes to preserve its authority, and its need not to confuse politics as the enactment of broad principles with day-to-day politics, where a multiplicity of practical compromises may be made in the quest for power.

NOTES

INTRODUCTION

1. Vali Nasr, *The Shia Revival: How Conflicts Within Islam Will Shape the Future*, New York: Norton, 2006.
2. In the words of King Abdallah II of Jordan, quoted in Robin Wright and Peter Baker, "Iraq, Jordan see threat to elections from Iran", *The Washington Post*, 8 December 2004.
3. The principal analyses taking this line are Graham Fuller and Rend Rahim Francke, *The Arab Shiʻa: The Forgotten Muslims*, New York: Palgrave, 1999; and Yitzhak Nakash, *Reaching for Power: The Shiʻa in the Modern Arab World*, Princeton University Press, 2008.
4. François Thual, *Géopolitique du chiisme*, Paris: Arléa, 2002.

1. THE CLERGY: A KEY ELEMENT

1. This interpretation is suggested by Juan Cole, *Sacred Space and Holy War: The Politics, Culture and History of Shiite Islam*, London: I.B. Tauris, 2002, in Chapter 3, "Rival Empires of Trade and Shiism in Eastern Arabia", pp. 32–37.
2. Yitzhak Nakash, *The Shiʻis of Iraq*, Princeton (NJ): Princeton University Press 2003 (1st edn 1994), pp. 25–48.
3. The word *imam* refers in this context simply to those who lead prayers in the mosques.
4. Houchang E. Chehabi, *Iranian Politics and Religious Modernism: The Liberation Movement of Iran Under the Shah and Khomeini*, London: I.B. Tauris, 1990.
5. The Pasdaran, also known as the Revolutionary Guard, served initially as a kind of praetorian guard for the regime. As will be seen

below, they quickly acquired a central role in the Islamic Republic's foreign policy.
6. This contrasts with its use in the Turkish-speaking world, where it was used as a title applicable to clerics.

2. TRANSNATIONAL NETWORKS

1. Magnus Ranstorp, (*Hizb'allah in Lebanon: The Politics of the Western Hostage Crisis*, Basingstoke: Palgrave Macmillan: 1997, p. 27), portrays Fadlallah as a full member of al-Da'wa. On the other hand, Jamal Sankari, (*Fadlallah: The Making of a Radical Shia Leader*, London: Saqi, 2005, p. 76) takes the view that Fadlallah was never an official member of the party.
2. In Iraq, Mohammed Redha al-Ghurayfi is a significant personality on the political and religious scene. As an associate of al-Sistani, he participated in the committee that re-drafted the Iraqi constitution adopted in 2005 and was appointed imam of Najaf's Imam Ali mosque, the city's principal religious institution.
3. The expression "sheikh" refers to religious scholars who have not risen to the level of being able to undertake *ijtihad*, or independent interpretation of religious texts.
4. The Arabic expression *ja'fari* refers to the Shia school of religious law. It is derived from the name of the sixth Imam, Ja'far al-Siddiq (who died in 765), who codified Shia jurisprudence.
5. There is also a Shia population in Abu Dhabi, though this is much smaller in size.
6. The best known instance was the *fatwa* he asked Musa al-Sadr in 1973 on this very subject.
7. The name derives from that of the Imam Hussein.
8. The 1943 National Pact was in practice the outcome of an informal conversation between the President of the Republic, the Maronite Bishara al-Khuri, and the Prime Minister, Riyadh al-Solh.
9. An estimate made by the CIA in 1986 suggested that the Shias made up 41 per cent of the population, the Sunnis 27 per cent, and the Maronites 16 per cent. See *Country Studies* (Federal research Division of the Library of Congress) www.country-studies.com/lebanon/population.html.

3. THE ISLAMIC REPUBLIC OF IRAN: A DISPUTED MODEL

1. This gave rise to the controversy known as the "Iran-Contra affair", when the sales were at last revealed to the international media by radical factions within the Iranian regime.

2. "Eurodif" was the name of a plant built in France for the enrichment of uranium of which the Shah had become a shareholder, having provided a loan for its construction, in exchange for which Iran acquired shares and rights to a proportion of the enriched uranium produced. After the revolution, Iran demanded the repayment of the loan and to continue to exercise its rights as a shareholder and to claim part of its output of enriched uranium. France rejected these demands.
3. "Imam" signifies "guide" in both Arabic and Persian.
4. The change of name occurred together with the party's recognition of the *marja'iyya* of Ali al-Sistani. This issue is highly significant in the current development of Shia political Islam and will be discussed below.
5. See Fouad Ibrahim, *The Shi'is of Saudi Arabia*, London: Saqi, 2006, p. 145. Fouad Ibrahim was a member of the Shirazist organisation in Saudi Arabia, the "Organisation for the Islamic Revolution in the Arabian Peninsula".
6. The status of *mujtahid* implies the achievement of *ijtihad*, in other words the ability to interpret religious texts independently.
7. Like all the Gulf monarchies, with the exception of Saudi Arabia, the archipelago of Bahrain had for a long period been a British protectorate. In 1971, when Bahrain gained independence, Iran issued a territorial claim, pointing out that it had been an Iranian possession up to the eighteenth century. A United Nations emissary went to Bahrain to hold consultation with the population on the issue, coming to the conclusion that by a large majority the inhabitants of Bahrain did not wish to be part of Iran.

4. THE POST SADDAM ERA

1. Vali Nasr, "Regional Implications of Shi'a Revival in Iraq", *The Washington Quarterly*, vol. 27 no. 3, Summer 2004, p. 20.
2. To use the felicitous expression coined by Philippe Droz-Vincent, *Vertiges de la puissance: Le "moment américain" au Moyen-Orient*, Paris: La découverte, 2007.
3. On the issue of the students' stipends, see Mehdi Khalaji, "The Last Marja: Sistani and the End of Traditional Religious Authority in Shiism", The Washington Institute for Near East Policy, Policy Focus no. 59, September 2006; and Babak Rahimi, *Ayatollah Sistani and the Democratization of Post-Baathist Iraq*, United

States Institute of Peace, Special Report no. 187, June 2007, p. 22 footnote 14.
4. Pierre-Jean Luizard, "The Sadrists in Iraq: challenging the United States, the Marja'iyya and Iran", in Sabrina Mervin (ed.) *The Shi'a Worlds and Iran*, London: Saqi Books/Beirut: IFPO, 2010, p. 276.
5. In the Arab Muslim context, "liberal" means "non-Islamic activist".
6. Vali Nasr, *The Shia Revival*, op. cit., p. 235.
7. The site of the Bahrain Center for Human Rights (www.bahrainrights.org/files/albandar.pdf) offers a download of the Bandar report but this is not always reliable (though a download was successful on 27 May 2011). The Bahraini government carefully monitors the web, where many opposition organisations give expression to their views.
8. I borrow this excellent expression from Perry Anderson, "On the Concatenation in the Arab World", *New Left Review*, no. 68, March-April 2011, pp 5–15.
9. www.saudiaffairs.net (accessed on 28 May 2011).
10. Such victories were claimed in May 2000, at the time of the Israel withdrawal from southern Lebanon, and again after Israel's attack on Lebanon in 2006, when there was no decisive Israeli victory and which enhanced the prestige of Hezbollah's struggle against the "Zionist entity".
11. Yaroslav Trofimov, "Saudi Shiites May See Gains from U.S. Invasion of Iraq", *Wall Street Journal*, 3 February 2003. Article available at http://www.sullivan-county.com/x/saudi_shiite.htm (accessed on 28 May 2011).
12. A school of Islamic law is known as a *madhhab*, of which there are officially four in Sunni Islam. Those who seek the normalisation of Shiism within Islam maintain that the Ja'fari Shia school is the fifth *madhhab* of Islam.
13. Crown Prince Abdallah became king in 2005 on the death of King Fahd, who had been incapacitated since suffering a stroke in 1995.
14. I am indebted to Nabil Mouline who drew my attention to the direct link between these events and the struggle between the King and the Sudayris.
15. "Hizbollah, Rebel without a Cause?", *International Crisis Group*, Middle East Briefing, 30 July 2003, p. 7.
16. Parliament is made up in total of 128 seats.
17. Waddah Sharara, *Dawlat Hezbollah: Lubnan Mujtama'an Islamiyyan* (The Hezbollah State: Lebanon, an Islamic Society), Beirut, Dar al-Nahr, 2006 (4th edn).

CONCLUSION

1. "Babism" was a religious movement which formed around Ali Mohammed (1829–1850), who claimed to have direct access to the divine message and presented himself as equal to the Prophet Mohammed. He was executed by the Shah in 1850. Several religious movements were subsequently based on Babism, of which Bahaism was one.
2. Peter Harling and Hamid Yassin Nasser, "The Sadrist Trend: Class Struggle, Millenarianism and Fitna", in Sabrina Mervin (ed.), *The Shi'a Worlds and Iran*, London: Saqi Books/Beirut IFPO, 2010.

BIBLIOGRAPHY

This bibliography includes the main works dealing with the subjects covered in this book, including books and articles mentioned in footnotes. No references are given to newspaper articles or to chapter titles in collective works, for which only the title of the book is given.

Adelkhah, Fariba, Jean-François Bayart and Olivier Roy, *Thermidor en Iran*, Paris: Complexe, 1993.

Ajami, Fouad, *The Vanished Imam. Musa al-Sadr and the Shia of Lebanon*, London: I.B. Tauris, 1986.

Akhavi, Shahrough, *Religion and Politics in Contemporary Iran: Clergy-State Relations in the Pahlavi Period*, Albany: State University of New York Press, 1980.

Alagha, Joseph, *The Shifts in Hizbullah's Ideology: Religious Ideology, Political Ideology, and Political Program*, Amsterdam: Amsterdam University Press, 2006.

Arjomand, Said Amir, *The Turban for the Crown: the Islamic Revolution in Iran*, Oxford: Oxford University Press, 1988.

Arjomand, Said Amir, *The Shadow of God and the Hidden Imam: Religion, Political Order and Societal Change in Shi'ite Iran from the Beginning to 1890*, Chicago: Chicago University Press, 1984.

Bakhash, Shaul, *The Reign of the Ayatollahs: Iran and the Islamic Revolution*, London: I. B. Tauris, 1985.

Buchta, Wilfried, *Who Rules Iran? The Structure of Power in the Islamic Republic*, The Washington Institute for Near East Policy and the Konrad Adenauer Stiftung, 2000.

Chehabi, Houchang E. (ed.), *Distant Relations: Iran and Lebanon in the Last 500 Years*, Oxford: Centre for Lebanese Studies, I. B. Tauris, 2006.

BIBLIOGRAPHY

Chehabi, Houchang E., *Iranian Politics and Religious Modernism: The Liberation Movement of Iran Under the Shah and Khomeini*, London: I.B. Tauris, 1990.

Cole, Juan R. I., *Sacred Space and Holy War: The Politics, Culture and History of Shiite Islam*, London: I.B. Tauris, 2002.

Cole, Juan R. I. and Nikki R. Keddie (eds), *Shi'ism and Social Protest*, New Haven: Yale University Press, 1986.

Djalili, Mohammed Reza, *Diplomatie islamique. Stratégie internationale du khomeynisme*, Paris: PUF, 1989.

Fandy, Mamoun, *Saudi Arabia and the Politics of Dissent*, London: Macmillan, 1999.

Fisher, Michael M. J., *Iran: from Religious Dispute to Revolution*, Cambridge (Mass.): Harvard University Press, 1980.

Fuller, Graham and Rend Rahim Francke, *The Arab Shi'a: The Forgotten Muslims*, New York: Palgrave, 1999.

Halm, Heinz, *The Shiites: A Short History*, Princeton: Markus Wiener Publishers, 2007.

Hamzeh, Ahmad Nizar, *In the Path of Hezbullah*, Syracuse (NY): Syracuse University Press, 2004.

Harik, Judith Palmer, *Hezbollah: the Changing Face of Terrorism*, London: I.B. Tauris, 2004.

International Crisis Group, *Hizbollah and the Lebanese Crisis*, Middle East Report no. 69, 10 October 2007.

International Crisis Group, *Hizbollah. Rebel without a Cause?* Middle East Briefing no. 7, 30 July 2003.

Ibrahim, Fouad, *The Shi'is of Saudi Arabia*, London: Saqi, 2006.

Jabar, Faleh A., *The Shi'ite Movement in Iraq*, London: Saqi, 2000.

Katzman, Kenneth, *The Warriors of Islam: Iran's Revolutionary Guards*, Boulder (CO): Westview Press, 1993.

Khalaji, Mehdi, *The Last Marja: Sistani and the End of Traditional Religious Authority in Shiism*, The Washington Institute for Near East Policy, Policy Focus, no. 59, September 2006.

Keddie, Nikkie R., *Modern Iran: Roots and Results of Revolution*, New Haven: Yale University Press, 2003.

Al-Khalidi, Sami Nasir, *Al-Ahzab al-Siyasiyya al-Islamiyya fi al-Kuwayt: al-Shi'a, al-Ikhwan al-Muslimin, al-Salafiyya* [The Islamic Political Parties in Kuwait: The Shi'a, the Muslim Brotherhood, the Salafis], Kuwait, Dar al-naba lil-nashra wa al-tawzi, 1999.

Al-Kharsan, Salah, *Hizb al-Da'wa al-Islamiyya: Haqa'iq wa watha'iq*

BIBLIOGRAPHY

[The Islamic al-Da'wa Party: Facts and Documents], Damascus: Al-mu'assasa al-'arabiyya lil-Dirasat wa al-buhuth al-istratijiyya, 1999.

Khosrokhavar, Farhad and Olivier Roy, *Comment sortir d'une révolution religieuse*, Paris: Seuil, 1999.

Khuri, Fuad I., *Tribe and State in Bahrain*, Chicago: Chicago University Press, 1980.

Kramer, Martin (ed.), *Shi'ism, Resistance and Revolution*, Boulder CO: Westview Press, 1987.

Litvak, Meir, *Shi'i Scholars of Nineteenth Century Iraq: The 'Ulama' of Najaf and Karbala'*, Cambridge: Cambridge University Press, 1998.

Luizard, Pierre-Jean, *La formation de l'Irak contemporain. Le rôle politique des ulémas chiites à la fin de la domination ottomane et au moment de la création de l'Etat irakien*, Paris: Editions du CNRS, 1991.

Louër, Laurence, *Transnational Shia Politics: Religious and Political Networks in the Gulf*, London: Hurst/New York: Columbia University Press, 2008.

Marschall, Christin, *Iran's Persian Gulf Policy: From Khomeini to Khatami*, London: Routledge/Curzon, 2003.

Mermier, Franck and Elizabeth Picard (eds), *Liban: Une guerre de 33 jours*, Paris: La Découverte, 2007.

Mervin, Sabrina (ed.), *The Shi'a Worlds and Iran*, London: Saqi Books/Beirut: IFPO, 2010.

Moslem, Mehdi, *Factional Politics in Post-Khomeini Iran*, New York: Syracuse University Press, 2002.

Nakash, Yitzhak, *Reaching for Power: The Shi'a in the Modern Arab World*, Princeton: Princeton University Press, 2006.

Nakash, Yitzhak, *The Shi'is of Iraq*, Princeton: Princeton University Press, 2003 (first edition 1994).

Nasr, Vali, *The Shia Revival: How Conflicts within Islam Will Shape the Future*, New York: Norton, 2006.

Norton, Augustus Richard, *Hezbollah: A Short History*, Princeton: Princeton University Press, 2007.

Norton, Augustus Richard, *Amal and the Shi'a: Struggle for the Soul of Lebanon*, Austin (TX): University of Texas Press, 1987.

Picard, Elizabeth, *The Lebanese Shi'a and Political Violence*, United Nations Research Institute for Social Development, Discussion Paper 42, April 1993.

Qassem Naim, *Hizbullah: The Story from Within*, London: Saqi, 2005.

BIBLIOGRAPHY

Rahim, Babak, *Ayatollah Sistani and the Democratization of Post-Ba'athist Iraq*, United States Institute of Peace, Special Report no. 187, June 2007.

Ranstorp Magnus, *Hizb'allah in Lebanon: The Politics of the Western Hostage Crisis*, Basingstoke: Macmillan, 1997.

Al-Rasheed, Madawi, "The Shi'a of Saudi Arabia: A Minority in Search of Cultural Authenticity", *British Journal of Middle Eastern Studies*, vol. 25, no. 1, May 1998.

Ra'uf, Adel, *Al-'Amal al-Islami fi al-'Iraq bayna al-Marja'iya wa al-Hizbiyya: Qira'a Naqdiya li-Masira Nusf Qarn 1950–2000* [Islamic Action in Iraq: between Marja'iyya and Parties: a critical reading of half a century], Damascus: Al-Markaz al-'Iraqi li al-I'lam wa al-Dirasat, 2000.

Ra'uf, Adel, *Muhammad Muhammad Sadiq al-Sadr: marja'iyyat al-maydan. Mashru'hu al-taghyiri wa watha'iq al-ightiyal*, [Mohammed Sadiq al-Sadr: the Popular Marja'iyya. His Plan for Change and Documents on his Assassination], Damascus: al-Markaz al-'Iraqi li al-I'lam wa al-Dirasat, 1999.

Ra'uf, Adel, *'Iraq bila qiyadah: qira'h fi azmat al-qiyada al-Islamiya al-Shi'iyya fi al-'Iraq al-hadith* [Iraq with No Direction: An Interpretation of the Crisis of Shia Leadership in Contemporary Iraq], Damascus: Al-Markaz al-'Iraqi li al-I'lam wa al-Dirasat, 2003.

Richard, Yann, *L'islam chiite*, Paris: Fayard, 1991.

Richard, Yann, "Ayatollah Kashani: Precursor of the Islamic Republic?", in Nikki Keddie (ed.), *Religion and Politics in Iran: Shiism from Quietism to Revolution*, New Haven: Yale University Press, 1983.

Roy, Olivier, "The Crisis of Religious Legitimacy in Iran", *The Middle East Journal*, vol. 53, no. 2, Spring 1999.

Saad-Ghorayeb, Amal, *Hizbu'llah: Politics and Religion*, London: Pluto Press, 2002.

Sankari, Jamal, *Fadlallah: The Making of a Radical Shi'ite Leader*, London: Saqi, 2005.

Sharara, Waddah, *Dawlat Hizbullah: Lubnan Mujtama'an Islamiyyan* [The Hezbollah State: Lebanon, an Islamic Society], Beirut, Dar al-Nahar, 2006 (fourth edition).

Thual, François, *Géopolitique du chiisme*, Paris: Arléa, 2002.

INDEX

Abadan, 54
Abd al-Samad, Adnan, 37, 62–63, 127
Abd al-Wahhab, Muhammad ibn, 35
Abdallah (King of Saudi Arabia), 110–112, 141 n2, 144 n13
Afsharids, 7
Ahmadinejad, Mahmud, 80, 84, 90, 136–138
Alawi (al-), 42
Alawi (al-), Mohammed, 54
Ali, 3–4, 6, 8, 11, 23, 142 n2
Ansari, Murtadha, 9
ARAMCO, 107
Assad (al-), Hafez, 41
Asefi (al-), Mohammed Mahdi, 38, 68
Ashur, Saleh, 41
Ashura, ix-x, 34, 55
Askari (al-), Murtada, 68
Association of Ulama of Najaf, 29
Awda (al-), Salman, 105
Azerbaijan, 42, 73

Baghdad, 3, 7, 13, 91, 104, 108–109, 136
Bahrain, 2, 6–7, 29, 31–35, 39–45, 53–55, 59, 64, 71, 80–81, 94–105, 108, 113, 127, 129, 131–133, 143 n7, 144 n7

Baath/Baathist, 11, 40, 44, 66–67, 87, 89–93
Bandar (al-), Saleh, 100–101, 144 n7
Basra, 30–31, 39, 84
Baz, Abd al-Aziz ibn, 105
Bazargan, Mehdi, 24, 53
Beheshti, Mohammed, 47
Berri, Nabih, 48, 56–57, 116
Bneid al-Gar, 41
Britain, 68, 81
British, 10, 14, 17, 20, 97, 100, 143 n7
Burujerdi, Muhammad, 20
Bush, George W., 83, 108
Buyids, 7

Carmathian(s), 6–7
Central Asia, 2, 45
Chamran, Mostafa, 24
Chirac, Jacques, 118

Da'wa (al-), 15–16, 18, 20–21, 28–33, 36–39, 42–46, 52, 54, 56–57, 60–62, 64, 66–68, 77–78, 81, 86–88, 92, 97, 99, 126–127, 132, 136, 142 n1
Da'wa (al-) al-Islamiyya (Basra Line), 14, 31
Damascus, 40, 63, 118
Dubai, 34, 39

INDEX

Fadlallah, Mohammed Hussein, 29–30, 33, 57, 60, 77–78, 142 n1
Fatima, 3, 6, 10, 34, 76
France, 21, 23, 59, 64, 118, 143 n2

Gaddafi regime, 47
Ghurayfi (al-), Abdallah, 33, 39, 142 n2
Gotbzadeh, Sadeq, 24

Ha'iri (al-), Kadhem, 68, 136
Hakim (al-), Abd al-Aziz, 65
Hakim (al-), Mahdi, 15–16, 39
Hakim (al-), Mohammed Baqir, 65
Hakim (al-), Muhsin, 14–16, 21, 29, 36, 39, 65
Hammad (al-), Ghalib, 111
Haqq (al-), 96, 100, 103, 131–132
Harb, Raghib, 57
Hariri (al-), Rafiq, 84, 118–120
Hasa, 34, 111
Hassan (Imam), 12–13
Hassan (al-), Hamza, 107
Hashemi (al-), Mahmud, 68
Hashemi, Mehdi, 54, 70–71
Hawali (al-), Safar, 105
Hezbollah, x, 29–30, 49, 55–56, 58–65, 77–78, 84, 93, 98–99, 104, 109, 111, 114–123, 126, 134, 144 n10
Hezbollah in the Hijaz, 61–62
Hijaz, 10, 61–62, 111
Hufuf, 111
Hussein, ix-x, 8, 12–13, 34, 40, 142 n7

India/Indian, 2, 8
Iran/Iranian(s), xi-xii, 1–3, 7–14, 16–17, 19–25, 33–34, 38, 40, 42, 44–48, 51–62, 64–71, 73–81, 83–97, 99, 103–104, 108–109, 111, 114, 116, 119, 121–122, 125–126, 129, 133–138, 142 n1, 143 n2, 143 n7

Iran-Contra Affair, 69, 142 n1
Iraq/Iraqi(s), ix, 1–2, 8, 10–11, 13–15, 17, 19–21, 24–25, 28–31, 33, 37–39, 40–42, 44, 46–48, 53–55, 58–60, 64–73, 81, 84–94, 99–100, 104–105–106, 108–110, 114, 123, 125–126, 133, 136, 142 n2
Islamic Amal, 56–57, 126
Islamic Enlightenment Society, 31–32
Islamic National Alliance, 63
Israel, 22, 57–60, 109, 114–115, 119–122, 144 n10
Israeli, 57, 114–116, 121–122, 144 n10

Ja'fari (al-), Ibrahim, 68, 86
Jabal Amil, 6–7, 29–30, 45, 47
Jamal, Abd al-Muhsin, 37, 62, 142 n1
Jamkaran, 137
Jordan, 10, 58, 121, 141 n2

Karbala, ix, 8, 12, 17–18, 39–42, 44, 73, 80
Kashani, Abu al-Qasim, 20
Khalifa (Al), 35, 43, 54, 97, 101–102
Khalifa (Al), Hamad bin Isa, 96
Khamenei, Ali, 60, 63–65, 68, 71, 74–79, 85, 88–89, 93, 99, 122, 134–135, 138
Khobar, 61
Khomeini, Ruhollah, x, xii, 6, 11, 18–24, 26, 51–53, 55, 57–58, 60–62, 64, 66, 68, 70–75, 79, 81, 85, 88
Khoei (al-), Abd al-Majid, 91
Khoei (al-), Abu al-Qasim, 11, 45, 91, 99
Khuweildi (al-), Hassan, 44
Khuzistan, 22, 53

INDEX

Kurani (al-), Ali, 30–31, 36–39, 47
Kuwait, 2, 29–30, 34, 36–38, 41–45, 62–64, 70, 77, 105–106, 127–128

Lahoud, Emile, 118
Lebanon, 1–2, 6, 12, 22, 29–30, 34, 40, 43, 45, 47–48, 54–62, 64–65, 77–78, 84–85, 93, 104, 109, 113–123, 126, 134–135, 144 n10
Beirut, 57, 75, 116

Ma'tuk (al-), Hussein, 63, 127
Madani (al-), Abdallah, 31
Madani (al-), Suleiman, 31
Mahdi (twelfth Imam), xi, 4, 61, 135, 137–138
Mahdi (al-), Yusuf, 44
Mahfuz (al-), Mohammed, 128
Maliki (al-), Nuri, 68, 86, 104
Manama, 42, 102
Mecca, 61
Medina, 61–62, 112
Mesopotamia, 8–11, 45, 72
Mohammedawi, Abd al-Karim, 65
Mohtashemi, Ali Akbar, 58
Montazeri, Hussein Ali, 53, 70, 74, 76
Montazeri, Mohammed, 54
Mosaddeq, Mohammed, 19–20
Mottahari, Morteza, 23
Movement for the Liberation of Iran (MLI), 24–25, 58
Movement of the Deprived, 12, 30, 48–49, 115
Mshaima, Hassan, 103, 132
Mudarrisi (al-), Hadi, 42–43, 47, 54, 70–71, 80
Mudarrisi (al-), Mohammed Taqi, 18, 41–42, 54, 70–71, 80
Mohammed (Prophet), ix, xii, 3, 5, 34, 145 n1
Musawi (al-), Hussein, 56–57

Najaf, 7–11, 13–15, 17, 20–21, 27–33, 35, 39–40, 42, 44–46, 52, 75–76, 89, 91–92, 95, 99, 104, 128, 131, 138, 142 n2
Najafi (al-), Mohammed Hassan, 9
Najati (al-), Hussein, 132
Nejd, 35
Naqi (al-), 36–38
Nasrallah, Hassan, 64

Oman, 2, 34, 41, 44

Pahlavi, 19, 21, 46
Pakistan, 34, 42
Palestine Liberation Organisation (PLO), 22, 43, 58
Palestinian(s), 22, 54, 57, 59–60, 114
Pasdaran, xi, 24, 54, 57–58, 65, 76, 87, 90, 93, 141 n5

Qa'ida (al-), 83
Qajar, 8
Qasim, Abd al-Karim, 14
Qasim, Isa, 32–33, 64, 99, 129
Qasim, Naim, 30
Qatif, 43, 55, 110–111
Qom, 7, 10–11, 13, 20–21, 44–47, 61–64, 66, 71, 74–76, 89, 93, 95–97, 99, 111, 127–128, 133, 136–137
Qumi, Hussein, 46

Rafsanjani (Hashemi-), Ali Akbar, 70, 80, 84
Redha (al-), Ali, 11
Risaliyyin, 92
Ruba'i (al-), Muwaffaq, 68

Sabah (Al), 36, 38, 63
Sadr (al), 45, 47, 90–91, 136
Sadr (al-), Mohammed Baqir, 15–16, 18, 26, 29, 33, 37, 39, 45–46, 52, 90

153

INDEX

Sadr (al-), Mohammed Sadiq, 46, 90–91, 93, 136
Sadr (al-), Muqtada, 46, 65, 90–93, 136–138
Sadr (al-), Musa, 12, 26, 30, 45–49, 56, 115, 126, 142 n6
Sadr City, 91
Sadrists, 90–94, 104, 136
Safavids, 7, 23
Saffar (al-), Hassan, 43–44, 54, 106–111, 113, 128
Salim, Azz al-Din, 39
Salman, Ali, 98–100, 104, 129–131
Sanad, Mohammed, 94–96
Saud (Al), 10, 35, 54–55, 62, 105–106, 108–111
Saudi Arabia, 2, 6, 34–35, 40–41, 43–44, 53–55, 58–59, 61–62, 64, 70–71, 103, 105–112, 121, 128, 143 n5/7
Sarkhu, Nasir, 37
Sayyida Zaynab, 33, 40–41, 71
Seif (al-), Fawzi, 44
Seif (al-), Tawfiq, 44, 128
Shah, 17, 19–22, 24, 38, 51–52, 58, 73, 96, 143 n2, 145 n1
Shams al-Din, Mohammed Mahdi, 29–30, 46
Sharaf al-Din, 45, 47
Sharaf al-Din, Abd al-Hussein, 46–47
Shariati, Ali, 12, 22–24, 129
Shariat-Madari, Mohammed Kazem, 73–74
Sharjah, 39, 42
Shayeb (al-), Ja'far, 110
Shebaa farms, 115, 120
Shirazi (al-), Hassan, 18, 40–41, 71
Shirazi (al-), Mohammed, 17–18, 26, 41–45, 47, 52, 54, 71–73, 76, 79, 95, 128, 133
Shirazi (al-), Sadiq, 133
Shirazi, Mirza Hassan, 17
Shirazists, 18, 21–22, 39–45, 52–55, 59, 61–62, 67, 69–70, 77, 79–81, 95, 99, 105, 107, 133, 143 n5
Shukhus (al-), Hashim, 61
Sind, 34
Sistani (al-), Ali, 2, 13, 87–89, 91, 99–100, 104, 131–134, 136, 142 n2, 143 n4
Sistani (al-), Muhammad Redha, 131
Supreme Council for Islamic Revolution in Iraq (SCIRI), 65, 67, 86–88, 90, 92, 94
Syria, 4, 33, 40–41, 47, 58, 60, 71, 80, 84, 115, 118–121

Tabrizi, Jawad, 95
Taleqani, Mahmud, 24
Tashkiri (al-), Ali, 68
Teheran, 19, 46, 51, 57–58, 62, 66, 71, 78, 80–81, 86, 92–95, 98, 104, 121–122
Transjordan, 10
Tufayli (al-), Subhi, 30, 57
Tyre, 46–47

United Arab Emirates (UAE), 2, 29, 34, 39, 42, 102–103
United States, 2, 57, 59, 64, 83–84, 101, 103, 108–109, 118

Wifaq (al-), 33, 99–103, 127, 129–132

Ya'qubi (al-), Mohammed, 92
Yazbek, Mohammed, 57
Yemen, 4